New Ideas for Old Furniture

New Ideas For Old Furniture

Leslie Linsley

Photos by Jon Aron

Lippincott & Crowell, Publishers   New York

FIRST EDITION

Designed by Jon Aron

U.S. Library of Congress Cataloging in Publication Data

Linsley, Leslie.
 New ideas for old furniture.
 Bibliography: p.
 1. Furniture finishing. 2. Furniture—Repairing.
I. Title.
TT199.4.L57   684.1'044   79-24776
ISBN 0-690-01756-1
80 81 82 83 84 10 9 8 7 6 5 4 3 2 1

Contents

New Ideas for Old Furniture

Introduction

I am writing this book on Nantucket Island, Massachusetts, a historically preserved New England community. Early American and other period furniture abounds. Houses are often sold completely furnished, and the buyer of a two-hundred-year-old house may acquire a horde of treasures that need only a bit of wood filler or some refinishing to restore them to their original beauty.

Over the years, I have been able to find some furniture of this sort and have spent many pleasurable summer days amid stripping solution, dirty rags, and scraps of sandpaper in an effort to re-create a beautiful but damaged piece. I do this because I like living with a bit of history and bringing some of the past into the present. I enjoy thinking about the people who once sat at my writing desk before me, wearing the edges down to soft curves. The signs of use etched in that table are somehow comforting. The carved wooden ornamentation on the base attests to the fact that people could afford the time to do such handiwork.

The majority of us also have a variety of less romantic furniture, acquired in a number of ways. Perhaps you furnished your first home with a few pieces donated by relatives, supplemented by other pieces found at yard sales, thrift shops, or secondhand stores. What most of us find are not considered antiques. (Junk dealers are quite savvy and know what a piece even in deplorable condition should command.) It's not easy to find a real antique bargain these

days. But those worn-out, plain, often seemingly useless pieces of no particular vintage or style can offer the greatest challenge for transformation. And since much of the old furniture that has long been relegated to our attics and basements has functional merit, it is worth giving it a second look.

In order to revitalize such pieces, a good design idea is needed. How can you best paint a table for use on the patio? What can you do with an infant's dressing stand now that the baby is grown? These projects are not lessons in historic restoration. What we are concerned with is giving a piece new life, sometimes keeping the basic form but giving it a different style and often a different function. The seed cabinet made into a delicate holder for sewing supplies gives it purpose for you. Turning a beat-up headboard into a towel rack with a mirror transforms a castoff into a clever and useful decoration.

The projects here might borrow some tricks from the antiques trade, such as repairing the caned seat of a chair, but for the most part we will be converting old furniture that anyone might own into something useful and attractive. The projects are simple to do using materials that are available in your local stores or easily ordered by mail. I hope that each technique or design idea will suggest more such new ideas for old furniture.

Tips on Repairing and Preparing

Where to Look and What to Look For

The first place to look for a piece of furniture to revive is in your own home. Sometimes we overlook what is right in front of us, and the piece with the most potential goes unnoticed. Check the attic or basement, either yours or someone else's, for forgotten items. A friend once told me to go into her attic to see what I could find, sure that I wouldn't uncover much. Half of what you will see in this book had been banished to her attic.

If you are rummaging in antiques shops (I use the word "antiques" loosely) or considering the purchase of discarded pieces at a yard sale, the first thing you should ask yourself is, "Can I use it as is?" If not, try to decide, on the spot, if you can turn it into something you *can* use. I find that if I don't get an inspiration immediately, I won't when I get home. However, if the piece has a nice shape and the price is right you should probably buy it, even though you don't have a good idea at the moment. You can afford to have it sit until you are inspired.

Don't worry about the finish. Almost anything can be removed or covered up. There is almost no superficial scratch, gouge, or minor chip that can't be repaired quickly and easily with materials from the hardware store. If you've never done this type of makeover work before, you'll be amazed at the variety of "fixit" material to be discovered. You might use your own experience to evaluate the potential of a piece that seems very badly broken or disfigured. Thus, if you are a beginner you should probably look for a first project that is appealing but not too badly bruised. However, some alterations may not be as difficult as they might look. A table that has too much ornamentation, or a sideboard that would look better if the legs were cut off, can be altered even by a novice. Perhaps a bureau you like has an oversized mirror in poor condition attached to it. Check the back to see if the mirror can be removed in order to save the dresser for a crafting project.

Tips on Stripping

Almost any finish can be stripped away to expose the naked wood beneath. If you will be painting the furniture, the old finish does not have to be stripped. If you are planning to re-stain the wood, however, or restore it to its natural appearance, you will need to remove the old finish completely. For this purpose you will find many good solutions, one of which is Strypeeze, that can be used for all surfaces, including those that have been stained, varnished, painted, etc. All-purpose paint remover can be used on painted furniture, and you might find that a putty knife or dull scraper is an effective tool. Sometimes we suspect that what we've found may be made of a wood that is quite beautiful, in which case it would be a shame to cover it again.

In most cases it is difficult to determine what kind of finish was originally applied to a piece of furniture. If an all-purpose finish remover doesn't work, chances are your furniture has been shellacked. Shellac is a very common finish, since it can be applied easily and dries quickly. Although the word "varnish" is generally

used to describe the final finishing coat, the finish you'll be stripping is probably shellac rather than true varnish. In this case the best way to remove the finish is with steel wool and wood alcohol. If your finish can't be removed with wood alcohol, try mineral spirits or turpentine.

Wear a pair of rubber gloves and have plenty of rags handy when you begin. Work outside if you can, but if you must work indoors, spread lots of newspapers around and open a window. Pour the alcohol or other solvent into a shallow bowl. Saturate the steel wool in the liquid and spread it generously onto the wood surface. Continue to glop it on, rubbing as you go. The liquid will penetrate, and the finish should wipe away easily. For stubborn spots, you might find a dull scraper useful if the piece you're working on isn't an antique or if the wood isn't very soft and susceptible to gouging. For most jobs, however, scrubbing with ample applications of solvent as needed will suffice. One tip for stripping shellac: Shellac removers dry quickly. When the solvent dries, if the finish has not been entirely dissolved it will gum up. If this happens, don't panic. Simply pour on more solvent and continue rubbing with the steel wool.

Tips on Commercial Stripping

You may ask, "Why spend all that time and effort, much less deal with the mess, when I can take my piece to a commercial stripper?" These "dip and strip" places are springing up all over the country. Look in the Yellow Pages under Furniture Repairing and Refinishing; chances are there's one near you. The cost to have a piece of furniture stripped is quite reasonable, but commercial stripping is not the answer for all furniture.

Commercial stripping is done by immersing the entire piece in a vat of chemicals. This can ruin certain kinds of furniture. I am advised by our local stripper, for example, never to have a veneered piece stripped. A piece painted black is very difficult to dip and strip. Also, a piece that has been lacquered requires special care, which is often costly. Finally, the chemicals used loosen the glue that holds joints together. In the case of some types of furniture, such as chairs, the piece must be taken apart to be re-glued. Check the sturdiness of the object beforehand to judge whether or not it can withstand this treatment. When in doubt, ask the person in charge for an opinion.

For most furniture, commercial stripping is a wonderful solution, and I have had many different wooden pieces "taken down" quite successfully this way. The wood is usually quite smooth and needs only a final sanding in places. For furniture with a lot of carved ornamentation or spindles and turnings, commercial stripping is the only practical method. Most reputable strippers know a great deal about old furniture and can advise you of the best way to handle your furniture.

Tips on Paint Preparation

You don't have to strip a piece of furniture that will be painted. If it is possible to remove hinges and knobs without injuring the piece, do so. With some very old pieces it is often best to work on the wood around the hardware and to clean the hardware right on the piece.

Before painting, remove surface dirt with a mild detergent. Wax, which has probably been applied at some point, can then be removed by rubbing down all surfaces with mineral spirits and a rag. Turpentine will do the job also, but it is more expensive and has a stronger odor. If the piece has been painted, shellacked, or varnished you will have to give it an overall sanding to roughen the surface.

Run your hand over the entire surface of the wood. If you feel any bumps or imperfections, now is the time to correct them. Sand the bumps with a fine grade of sandpaper and fill in any nicks and gouges with wood putty. Wood putty is easy to use, especially the water-based kind, such as Elmer's Carpenter's Wood Filler. Use a putty or spackle knife or an old butter knife to apply it.

Let the piece dry, usually overnight, and sand it smooth. Wipe away all sand and wood dust before painting. Your careful preparation for painting will be evident in the smooth, lovely surfaces of the finished piece. If you start with a sloppy underbase, your finish will certainly reveal this. I am always tempted to rush through the preparation, but the process and the results are much more satisfying when the work is done properly. It really doesn't take that much more time to get the piece in shape to paint.

Before you can paint a metal piece, you will have to remove any rust that may have accumulated. Rust spots can be removed with a bit of hand sanding. If your piece is badly rusted, it will require a special rust-remover solution you can find in the hardware store. In addition, your metal furniture can be sanded with an electric sander or by hand. All traces of rust must be thoroughly removed before painting.

Tips on Sanding

When choosing the right abrasive for the job, remember that coarser grades will remove the most finish and finer grades are used for finishing work. There are different types and sizes of sandpaper for hand sanding, as well as pre-cut strips to fit sanding machines and sanding disks to fit drill adapters.

To remove a lot of paint or to smooth large rough areas, start with a coarse grit or grade of sandpaper. The number printed on the back of each sheet will tell you the grade. Generally, the higher the number, the finer the grit. *With each successive sanding, use a finer grade.* The finer grades create a smoother finish.

When using an electric finishing sander, insert the sandpaper or press on a strip of Press 'N Sand sandpaper and let the sander do the work. Turn the sander on before applying it to the wood, then move it slowly back and forth in wide overlapping arcs. Lift the sander off the surface before turning it off.

When removing an old paint or varnish finish without a chemical, use a coarse grade of sandpaper and go over the entire

surface. Don't concentrate in one small area before moving on to the next, or the finish in that spot will become heated and soft. If you have used a liquid remover first, be sure to clean the surface and wait for it to dry before sanding.

When using the electric sander, place it flat on the surface and avoid leaning on it, unless you are removing a particularly stubborn finish. Check the surface often to make sure you aren't removing more than you want. The new, lightweight tools are nearly effortless to work with, making the job fun rather than a chore.

If you have small flat areas to sand, you might invest in a sanding block. Made of lightweight plastic, it will fit comfortably in your hand. When used with a strip of sticky-backed sandpaper such as Press 'N Sand, it is perfect where careful, final sanding is required. Sand with the grain of wood, not against it, to avoid lifting wood fibers.

Tips on Chair Repair

Although many amateurs fix loose chair joints by pounding nails, screws, and iron angles into them, the experts agree that glue will hold a chair together far more effectively. Still, almost every old chair that I have retrieved had a nail or two pounded into its side.

To re-glue a loose joint, first clean away the old glue with hot water mixed with a little vinegar. Borden's white Elmer's Glue-All usually works with any wood repair job. However, their Elmer's Carpenter's Wood Glue is even stronger. It grabs faster on initial contact, yet allows the piece to be positioned for final clamping. It dries quickly, resists water, lacquers, and varnishes, and can be sanded and painted. Best of all, it can be cleaned off hands and tools with warm water. If you have loose corner joints or loose rungs that are difficult to clamp, make a tourniquet out of rope to hold the chair tightly together. It is essential that pressure be applied to the glued area until it is dry.

The joints of a chair that is stripped commercially will often become loose. It is not necessary to take the whole chair apart unless it is too rickety to bear a person's weight. If the chair is that far gone, you will need some expert advice on furniture repair. However, minor joint repairs are easily corrected with glue and clamps. If a leg or rung is broken, it is best to have a replacement made. Take the broken part to the hardware or lumber store in order to select a matching dowel.

Tourniquet holds chair while glue dries.

Tips on Repairing Veneer

If you've found a piece of furniture with part of the veneer missing, don't discard it as unusable before considering how it might be repaired. The veneer can be matched and replaced, which involves figuring out the type and approximate dimension of wood required and ordering the piece from a supplier who specializes in veneers. This is not expensive, but it is time-consuming and tricky, since we can't always be sure that the color and grain of the new piece will match the old veneer perfectly.

George Grotz, the famous "Furniture Doctor," recommends an ingenious, quick, and simple method for repairing small chipped areas. Select a wax crayon of the color nearest to the wood. Crumble the crayon into bits that will fit in a tablespoon, and melt it over the kitchen stove. Dribble the melted wax onto the area needing repair. Let the wax cool, and then use your putty knife to scrape it level. To protect the repaired area, apply a coat of shellac over the wax.

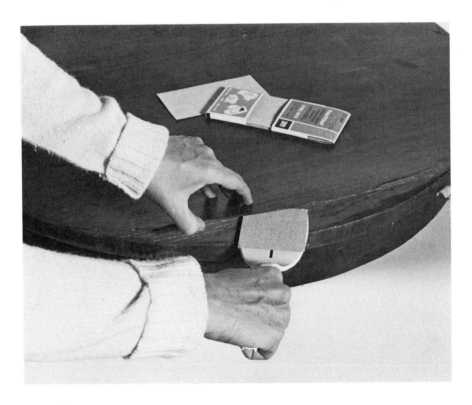

If you plan to paint the surface, and the gap in the veneer is not too large, you can fill it with wood putty. Simply glob it on with the putty knife and then wipe the excess away with the knife, re-applying until the surface is level. Let this dry before sanding the entire surface. If you plan to stain the veneer, however, do not use wood putty to make repairs, because the stain will not penetrate the wood filler.

If the veneer on a table has lifted at one corner, you needn't fear that the entire surface will peel away with a tug. Most likely, the veneer was glued down to stay for many years and has simply dried out in one area. There are two methods for repairing it.

Method One: Cover the problem area with waxed paper, and on top of that lay several sheets of newspaper. Set your iron on a low temperature and place it, warm side down, on top of the newspapers. Allow it to rest there for about ten minutes, but keep an eye on it so that the papers don't burn. Then, remove the iron and replace it with a heavy pile of books. Leave this overnight. The heat from the iron should have melted the glue, making it moist and adherent once again. If this hasn't happened, go on to Method Two.

Applying weight to veneer while glue dries.

Method Two: If the veneer is loose enough to pick up so that glue can be applied underneath, fine. If not, the loose piece must be cut off with a new razor blade and glued back on. Elmer's Carpenter's Wood Glue or Elmer's Glue-All works well. If the piece is replaced carefully, the cut mark will never show. Sand the area that will receive the veneer and, if possible, sand the underside of the piece of veneer itself before applying the glue to both surfaces. Set the loose piece in place and weight it down for several hours or overnight.

Since loss of moisture is the cause of buckling veneer, you can protect your veneered furniture from problems in the future by sealing veneered sections with a thin coating of varnish. In this case I coated the top and underside of the tabletop. Wood varnish for indoor furniture comes in semi-gloss or glossy finish and must be allowed to dry for twenty-four hours.

Clamping veneer while gluing.

Tips on Removing Veneer

Removing veneer is *not* a very simple task that can be accomplished in minutes. In many cases a corner of the veneer has buckled and come loose, but that doesn't mean the entire piece will lift off with a little prying. I find that flat tools, such as a putty knife and a chisel, are best. Insert under the veneer so that you can pry it off a little at a time. Once you have removed the veneer that can be lifted easily, soak the remaining veneer with a solution of warm water and vinegar. Pour this over the veneer and let it penetrate the wood surface to loosen the old glue. Continue to use your tools, taking care not to gouge the wood beneath the veneer. If this should happen and you are planning to paint over the surface, the depressions can be filled with wood putty. However, if you are

planning to stain the newly exposed surfaces, the stain may not penetrate these areas with one application. Two or three coats will achieve satisfactory results, however.

Once most of the veneer has been removed, you may find that planing the surface helps smooth off stubborn sections of veneer that refused to be separated during the just described process. A finishing sander will further smooth the surface as well as minimize any imperfections in the wood. This will provide you with a cleanly prepared area on which to proceed.

Sand the rest of the piece as well. For the curved surfaces or hard-to-get-at crevices, small pieces of sandpaper cut for hand sanding are best. Press 'N Sand, made by 3M, has a sticky backing and can be adapted for many uses. It is especially ideal for rolling around a dowel or pencil to get at areas that would otherwise be difficult to reach.

Tips on Brush Painting

Once your piece has been sanded and wiped clean of sand dust, and all imperfections have been filled, you are ready to paint. Enamel paint withstands wear better than latex or water-base paint. However, one or more outer coats of varnish will protect the latex paint finish adequately.

Begin by applying a primer coat of paint. You can purchase a special "primer" or "sealer," or you can use the paint you have selected as a primer coat. Dip your brush halfway into the paint and draw it up the rim so that the excess runs back into the can. For neatness and economy you can use a hammer and nail to pound three or four holes into the rim of the can once it is open. Then excess paint will run back into the can. Draw the brush in one direction across the surface you are painting. Try not to overload your brush in order to avoid drips and "rollover" (a buildup of paint at the edges of furniture). Paint should thin out as you draw your brush toward the outer edges. If you find that you end up with some drip marks on the painted surface, try to thin them out by going over them with the brush. If this tactic causes more mess, simply let the drips dry thoroughly and then sand and repaint.

Let the first coat of paint dry completely before sanding it lightly with a medium grade of sandpaper in preparation for the next coat. It is important to start each new coat with a clean brush. To clean brushes used for oil-base enamel paint, use turpentine or mineral spirits. When using latex or water-base paint, use mild soap and warm water to clean up. Latex paint dries quickly, and you can apply two or three coats in a day. Enamel paint is tougher and longer lasting, but it requires more patience to apply and takes twenty-four hours to dry.

Tips on Spray Painting

Why not simply spray paint everything? Paint that comes in spray cans has one big advantage: It is easy and quick to apply. However, the choice of colors is fairly limited. It is also more expensive than brush-applied paint and therefore usually more appropriate for small projects. Because the paint is thin and runs easily, certain precautions should be taken. Spray outdoors when possible, to avoid fumes and paint fallout on other areas. Stand ten to twelve inches away from the object to be painted. Shake the can vigorously. Then, holding the can upright, start spraying, keeping the can moving back and forth in a steady motion. Do not try to coat one area heavily before moving on to the next. Instead, cover the entire area with several thin sprayings. Let the paint dry. (Spray enamel dries quickly.) Allow any drips to dry, then sand them smooth and repaint. Continue to re-apply paint in the same way until the object is sufficiently coated.

Tips on Unwarping

Probably the most common problem of furniture that has been discarded or left in a damp basement is warping. I found a table that was a victim of warping, but since it was the exact size I wanted and had a nice base, it seemed worth working on. The tabletop was bowed so that the top center was higher than the rest, although the edges were a bit curled too. Most table leaves, if warped, curl upward, leaving a concave center.

A tabletop that is warped must be removed from its base. Begin by stripping off the old finish as described earlier. Then sand down the stripped surface so that the wood is free of residue. Do the unwarping outdoors. Place the tabletop or leaf convex side down and pour boiling water on the concave side. When it is well-soaked, turn the warped piece over. The curved side will dry in the sun, and in the process the piece will flatten out. This will take a few hours if the warping isn't too great, or several days if it is severe. Once the piece is unwarped, bring it indoors and let it dry out thoroughly. Coat both sides of the piece with shellac or varnish to keep it from warping again.

If you can't work outdoors, your radiator will have to substitute for the sun. Devise a way to prop the warped object a few inches above the radiator, with the concave side up. Place several wet rags on top of the piece, keeping them wet by pouring boiling water over them. If you don't have a radiator, use a furnace or hot air ducts.

Pineapple Table

This kind of table is fairly common, and you can probably find one similar to it. I uncovered this in a laundry room, barely visible under clothes and boxes of detergent. Because of its size and shape, it has a lot of design possibilities.

A recently applied coat of white paint could not hide the blue paint beneath. Once stripped of these two layers, a coat of green and patches of still another coat, yellow, emerged. It became evident that the best way to approach a piece of furniture like this, which has turnings and curves that have been painted several times, was to sand it and paint it one more time. It is best to use an electric sander to get the surface smooth enough to paint again. When furniture is old, the paint often flakes right off and sanding is not difficult.

The base and legs of this table are uninteresting, so I decided to minimize them with two coats of semi-gloss black enamel. This in turn gives emphasis to the top, which has a pleasing shape. For the top, I chose colors that contrast strongly with the black and match the room decor in which the table will be placed.

The decorative technique used on the tabletop is stenciling. The design has been transferred to the tabletop by applying paint to the wood surface through the perforations in a cut-out pattern, or stencil. When the cut-out template is removed, the pattern is descernible. A technique used extensively in America in the eighteenth and nineteenth centuries to decorate furniture, floors, walls, and accessories, stenciling is now enjoying a revival with modern craftworkers. The pineapple design used here is a popular traditional American design. You can make your own stencil or buy one pre-cut. Stenciling can be done on painted as well as raw wood, although a wooden surface that is slick or shiny should be sanded before stenciling.

Acrylic paint, available in art supply stores, is excellent for stenciling. It comes in every conceivable color, adheres to almost any surface, and can be used right from the tube. The color is permanent and washable. Use water to remove the paint from hands and brush.

Materials Needed: Design planned on paper, white latex wall paint, acrylic paint (one tube each Grumbacher Hansa Yellow Medium, Yellow Ochre Light, Cadmium Orange, Portrayt, Chromium Oxide Green, and Burnt Umber), bowl or paper bucket, two-inch-wide paintbrush, fine grade of sandpaper, cardboard, stencil paper, masking tape, stencil or X-Acto knife, tracing paper, stencil brush, semi-gloss or high-gloss indoor wood varnish, brush cleaner, fine steel wool, clear paste wax, soft cloth. (You can find the acrylic paint, stencil brush, paper, knife, and tracing paper in art supply stores.)

First plan your design on paper. If you decide to use the pineapple provided here, adjust the size (see page 146) to fit your surface, and position the paper design on your table to see where it will look best. You might go a step further by coloring it in with crayons or markers to get a rough idea of how the finished product will look.

The background paint used here is white latex wall paint tinted with two acrylic paint pigments. The entire project, once complete, will be given a protective coating or two of oil-base wood varnish.

Begin by mixing the pigments equally: Grumbacher acrylic Hansa Yellow Medium with Grumbacher Yellow Ochre Light. Then pour a small amount of the white latex paint into a bowl or paper paint bucket and add to it a little bit of the pigment mixture, creating a puddle of color in the white paint. Combine the two thoroughly to eliminate streaks of color running through the white paint. When the hue is consistent throughout, add this mixture to the larger amount of white paint. If you need to add more pigment, mix it into a small quantity of latex, as just described, before adding it to the larger amount of paint. You'll avoid the lumps and bumps in the paint that can form when the acrylic paint is added directly from the

Plan design on paper as a guide for stencils.

tube. It takes very little pigment to bring white up to a desired background color, so it is best to add the pigment a tiny bit at a time. Be sure to mix a large enough batch of tinted paint to cover your table surface with the necessary two or three coats. If you run out before the project is finished, you'll find that it is difficult to mix a new batch that will match the original exactly.

A two-inch-wide paintbrush is best for this job. Apply one coat of paint over the sanded and prepared tabletop, keeping the brush strokes going in one direction. This paint mixture will dry quickly. Sand the first coat slightly with fine sandpaper before giving the table another coat of paint, which should cover the area. If necessary, apply a third coat. Allow the final coat to dry and sand lightly once again.

Back your design with a protective piece of cardboard. Place the sheet of stencil paper, which is translucent, over the design and secure it with masking tape. Using a stencil knife or X-Acto knife, cut out each section of the design. The blade you use should be clean and sharp. When making the knife cuts, take care not to run

Stencil cuts easily with sharp blade.

over the edges with the knife, because paint will seep through these cuts when you're stenciling. You might find a pre-cut stencil that appeals to your sense of design, but the design possibilities are limitless if you create your own. You have the option of picking up part of a fabric design or shapes from wallpaper or anything else in the room that is not too intricate. The simpler the design, the more satisfactory the results will be.

Now you are ready to mix the colors to be used on the stencil. The burnt-orange hue of the pineapple comes from mixing Grumbacher's Cadmium Orange and Portrayt in equal amounts. The border around the pineapple is done in the same color. The pineapple leaves and leaf design in the border are created with a mixture of Chromium Oxide Green and a drop of Burnt Umber to tone it down. I've subdued the bright colors as they come from the tube by mixing pairs of them together in order to obtain hues that are more elegant and traditional in feeling. To make a dark color less intense, add a darker color. To make a light color more pastel, or less intense, add white. Once all your colors are mixed, you can begin to stencil.

Plan the placement of the border before you begin. In order to make sure that the border is aligned symmetrically with the shape of the table, make a freehand oval the size of the tabletop. Trace the

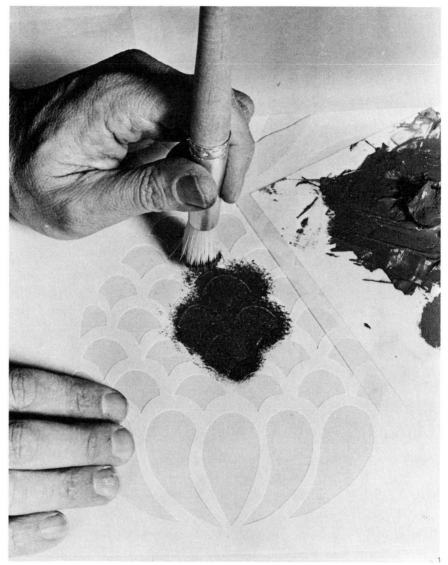

Results should have sharp edges.   *Hold stencil brush vertically and tap.*

border design provided here on one quarter of the oval. Take the tracing paper, flop it over, and trace the design on the opposite side so the border design joins and is continuous. Adjust the design if it doesn't fit perfectly. The sizes of the tables worked on will vary, so you'll need to adapt the dimensions of this particular design to fit your area.

Stencil the large design in the center of the stencil first. Tape the cut-out stencil to the area so that it is firmly in place. (Some stencil paper has a slightly sticky backing, which is excellent to help keep it in place.) This way there is no chance for the paint to seep under the cut-out area, and the stencil will stay crisp and clean. If you are using a pre-cut stencil sheet, you may find that you are using only part of the design. In this case, be sure to mask out the stencils you won't be using, so that you don't accidentally paint over a cut-out you don't want.

Always use a dry brush to stencil. If the paint is runny, it will surely seep under the stencil into areas not meant to receive paint. Dab the stencil brush on the paint. Hold the brush firmly in a vertical position and tap excess paint off onto a scrap piece of paper before beginning. It is best to have very little paint on the brush. Tap the brush up and down at the openings in the stencil design. Try to stencil from the outside of the design inward. Move from one area to another as the paint fills in the openings. Do not overload each area with paint. A small amount covers quite a bit of space. If an area hasn't been sufficiently covered, you can go over it again, after it is dry, in the same way.

When the body of the pineapple is completely covered, wash the brush thoroughly in hot water. Never let the paint dry on the brush. Squeeze the excess water out of the brush to get it as dry as possible before going on to stencil the leaves.

To do the leaves, tap the green color onto the leaf areas in the same way. Using a straight up-and-down motion, tap a tiny bit of color onto the surface. Continue to do this until the leaf cutouts are filled in.

When all cut-away areas have been filled in with color and the paint has dried, peel the stencil sheet away from the surface of the table. Your design should be perfect. You can now go on to the border design.

Since this is a delicate stencil, you'll need to take a bit more care when applying the paint. Again, tape the border design onto the surface and tap the paint onto the exposed table surface. In this case, you will have to keep picking up the stencil and moving it along as you do each section. To avoid smudging, be sure the paint is dry in each section before you place the stencil sheet down again. Acrylic paint dries quickly, so you should have very little waiting time. Once the border is complete, add details freehand or with a stencil where you feel they would look good. With the pineapple design, the small leaves add a touch of color and interest to the overall pattern.

Give the entire table—legs and base as well as the top—a coat of semi-gloss wood varnish. Polyurethane varnish is excellent to use on a surface that will get a lot of use. If you prefer a very shiny, wet look, select a high-gloss finish. Apply the varnish in long strokes beginning in the center of the table and working out to the edges. Do not overload your brush; a thin coat is best. The varnish will take twenty-four hours to dry. Once dry, a second coat is preferable, but if you don't want to put in the extra time, one coat will protect the stenciled design. Lightly rub over the entire piece with a piece of very fine steel wool. Give the table a coat of clear paste wax, buff with a soft rag, and you're finished.

Section of stenciled border.

Antique Glaze Mantelpiece

Glazing is an excellent way to create an antiqued effect. A glaze is a tinted transparent film made of color ground in oil and mixed with varnish. Glaze can be applied to furniture as well as to doors and molding trim to create an antique look. It is usually most effective on a very ornate piece with lots of carvings. You can make your own mixture by using equal parts of color, varnish, and mineral spirits. If you prefer, you can have the glaze prepared at a paint store. Since the shade can be mixed to harmonize with anything, take along a sample of your desired color. Perhaps you will want to glaze a piece of furniture to match your fabric or wallpaper. Usually glazes are mixed to achieve an earth tone, with raw umber as the base color. For a lighter and warmer tone, burnt sienna is used. Louise Coe created a wood-grain effect on her mantelpiece with an ochre color base to achieve the look of real oak.

Final panel of fireplace to be glazed.

Apply glaze in one direction.

Materials Needed: Sandpaper, flat white water-base paint, glaze (prepared at the paint store or by you with color, varnish, mineral spirits), two-inch-wide brush, steel wool, indoor wood varnish, brush cleaner, bowl with soapy water, very fine WetorDry sandpaper, clean soft cloth, very fine steel wool, furniture paste wax.

The surface to be glazed must first be sanded clean. Next apply two or three coats of white paint, preferably flat water-base paint. The glaze should be brushed over a small area at a time so that it does not dry before the desired effect has been achieved. If you are working on a mantelpiece, it is best to use a two-inch-wide flat brush. Always pull the brush in one direction when applying the glaze. Let the glaze set for five or ten minutes, then with a piece of fine steel wool lightly wipe across the glazed area to create the wood-grain effect. Wipe away most of the glaze from the large flat areas, such as panels, but leave it in the crevices, curves, and corners, where dirt and the signs of aging may have accumulated. Continue to work across the surface in this way, blending each small area into the next. Do not spend a lot of time going over each section. I find that the quicker I work, the better the results. It will take about fifteen minutes for the glaze to begin to dry. If you are unhappy with the results before the glaze is dry, you can wipe it away and re-apply where necessary.

When the glazing has been completed, let the piece dry thoroughly overnight. Apply a coat of varnish over the glaze to protect it and to give your piece a finished look. A good indoor wood varnish or polyurethane varnish is available in a satin,

Steel wool creates even grain effect.

semi-gloss, or glossy finish. The choice is up to you, but my recommendation for simulating the soft patina usually found on fine wood furniture is the satin finish. The varnish, which has an oil base, must be allowed to dry undisturbed for twenty-four hours. While there are some water-base, fast-drying varnishes on the market, they are not very good for this purpose.

During the drying time, dust particles may settle on the surface, causing it to be uneven. The beautiful smooth finish found on fine furniture can be achieved in the following way. Fill a small bowl with soapy warm water—you can use dishwashing detergent or hand soap for this. Soak a small piece of very fine WetorDry sandpaper in the water. Lightly stroke the varnished surface in the direction of the "grain," rewetting or replacing the sandpaper when necessary and wiping away the sand grit with a soft clean cloth as you work. The purpose of this is to smooth out imperfections without sanding away your antique effect. Next, rub lightly over the area with very fine steel wool. Grade 0000 is best; try a craft shop if your hardware store doesn't carry it. Do not apply too much pressure when rubbing with the steel wool. Finally, use a soft furniture paste wax to protect the smooth finish and make the wood surface glow.

Louise applied an antique finish to the molding and closet doors in her bedroom as well as to the slats of the old wooden venetian blinds, creating a rich oak-grained effect to match the mantelpiece. The blinds cover large windows that dominate an entire wall and are quite handsome.

A Down-on-the-Farm Chair

A child's school chair lends itself beautifully to many designs and crafting techniques. If you can't pick one up at a flea market, you can order one from a school furniture supplier. These chairs are inexpensive, sturdy, and not very pretty as is. Often they are stained from use in the classroom. This one was covered with ink and sloppily applied shellac. After a thorough cleaning with alcohol and a good overall sanding, it was ready to paint. If you have an old chair, it will need a primer coat of enamel, then two more coats of white paint. Since this type of furniture will get a lot of use, and possibly abuse, you should give it a good hard protective finish.

I took the design for this chair from a wallpaper motif in a child's room. By transferring designs in this way, you can customize a piece of furniture to match any decor. If you don't happen to be wallpapering a room, you might look for sample books from a wallcovering store. Often when wallpaper designs have been discontinued, some sample books are of no further use to the store and are there for the asking. The paper I used for this project is from the Wall-Tex collection. It is made of tough, easy-to-clean vinyl, and the design is delightful. The objects are cut out, pasted on the chair, and protected with many layers of varnish. This wallpaper is not expensive, and with the surplus left over from this project, you might consider decorating other pieces. This farm scene would look good on a dresser, a baby's crib, or a child's headboard. Such accessories as a lampshade, wastebasket, or toy box could be covered to match.

Old oak school chairs.

Materials Needed: Designs, cuticle scissors, Elmer's Glue-All, rubber brayer (or similar object, hard and cylindrical, like a paintbrush handle), sponge, razor blade, indoor wood varnish, two-inch-wide paintbrush or sponge brush, brush cleaner, very fine sandpaper, very fine steel wool, clear furniture paste wax, soft clean cloth.

Once the chair has been properly prepared and sanded smooth, determine where elements of the design should be placed by cutting them out and playing around with them on the decorating surface. If the design is very lacy or intricate, cuticle scissors are easiest to use. Also, if your background paint is not white, be sure to trim away the excess white paper around your cutouts. If you don't do this, the cutting will look messy and the white paper will show up on the colored background of the chair.

42

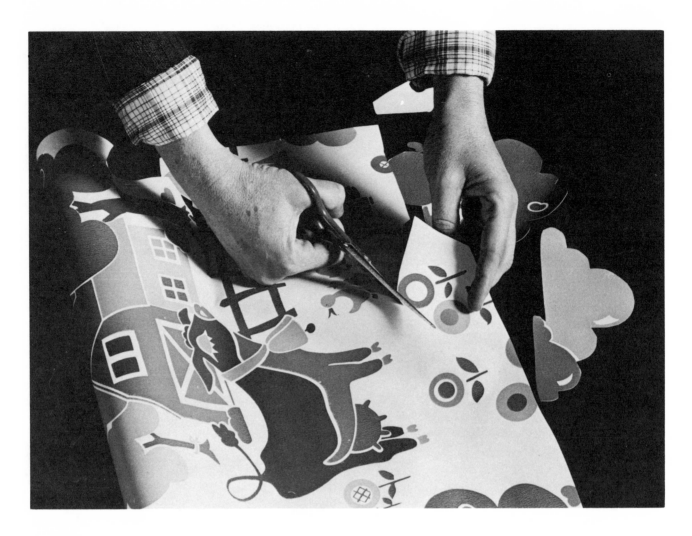

When you have decided where everything will be placed, lift
one cutout, apply Elmer's Glue-All to the back of it, and replace it
on the chair. Continue to do this until everything has been glued in
place. Since this paper is very thick, it was necessary to roll it down
securely. For this I used a rubber brayer, but any hard cylindrical
object will do; a paintbrush handle is fine. Roll the brayer over each
cutout so that the excess glue underneath oozes out at the edges.
Wipe this away with a damp sponge; if the glue is allowed to dry on
the furniture it may become discolored under the varnish. Go over
each cutout design again and again until you are sure there are no
air bubbles trapped beneath. If the edges curl up, lift them with a
razor blade and apply more glue to the sections that aren't sticking.
Let the designs dry on the chair for a few hours.

Next, varnish the entire object. For this project I used a
high-gloss varnish, which gives the chair a shiny, wet look. If the
design you have chosen is rather subdued and the chair more
traditional in style, you should use a satin or semi-gloss varnish.
The high gloss will give your piece a harder finish, however.

Begin varnishing in the center of the chair seat. The varnish will
form a small pool where the seat is recessed. Spread the varnish

outward to each edge. Do not add more varnish to your brush. A sponge brush, available in the hardware store, is excellent for varnishing because it will not cause streaking in the finish. It won't last as long as a good natural-hair brush, but it compensates for that by being quite inexpensive.

To seal out moisture, coat all other exposed surfaces, including the undersides of side rungs and the front seat lip. Since the varnish is transparent, it is easy to miss covering an area. Check to be sure the entire surface has been coated. When you think you are done, examine the chair from different angles to be sure you haven't missed a spot.

Leave the chair standing in an out-of-the-way place so that a minimum of dust particles will settle into the varnish. It will take twenty-four hours for each coat to dry thoroughly. Never, never apply another coat if the first is still tacky, or you will cause the whole thing to become gummy and it will never dry. Because the wallpaper cutouts are so thick, several coats of varnish are required to cover the cutout so that its surface is continuous with the surface of the chair. Each application takes about twenty minutes. Therefore, although it takes twenty-four hours for the varnish to dry, the

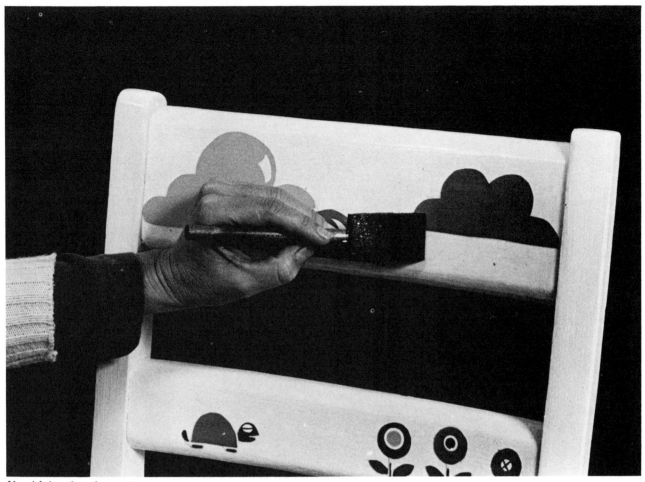

Varnish in a dust-free environment.

work involved takes only minutes each day. Between coats, keep the brush in a small can of brush cleaner (or mineral spirits or turpentine) to keep it from drying out. When the chair is ready to receive another coat of varnish, be sure to squeeze the excess cleaner from the brush before using it again.

Once you have applied three coats of varnish, you can sand the entire piece very lightly. Using very fine sandpaper, smooth the finish. Do not apply much pressure or you will sand away the surface of the design. Two or three more coats of varnish should do the trick. Again, sand the final coat very lightly, just enough to insure a smooth finish. For added smoothness, rub over all with very fine steel wool. (This is often difficult to find in a hardware store, but most craft shops carry the number 0000 steel wool that is best for this.)

For the final step, apply a thin coat of furniture paste wax to the chair. Let it stand for ten minutes before buffing with a soft clean cloth. This will protect the chair and give it a satiny finish. The piece will be totally child-proof—even crayon can easily be washed off. The tough varnish finish will not allow liquid spills of any sort to penetrate to the design surface.

Sitting Pretty

Once you have worked on one small, sturdy child's chair you will be inspired to experiment further. These chairs are a joy to decorate because the area to be covered is small and they look so much better than when left in the "raw." Because I started with three chairs, I thought it would be fun to design each with a different feeling. The farm scene is cheerfully fanciful, this design is delicate, and the striped motif (see "Colors to Sit On," next) is rather bold. If you would rather not put a lot of work into these chairs, you can still get quite attractive results by simply painting each a bright color, enhanced by a shiny coat of protective varnish.

The design element here is lace doilies from the five-and-ten, and the idea is to make the chair appear to have been printed with a lace design. Once several coats of varnish have been applied, the surface is as smooth as glass, with the doilies embedded beneath.

Materials Needed: Primer paint, fine sandpaper, white latex paint, one tube red acrylic paint, two-inch-wide paintbrush or sponge brush, enough paper doilies to cover piece, Elmer's Glue-All, bowl or paper cup, water, sponge, high-gloss indoor wood varnish (preferably polyurethane), brush cleaner, fine steel wool, clear paste wax.

Clean the chair of any sticky substance and check under the seat for dried-up gum. (I found a piece of untold vintage on one of the rungs.) Sand the chair until it is smooth. If a finish has already been applied, refer to the first section of this book to learn how to remove the old finish and prepare the piece for painting.

If you are planning to paint the chair with a dark background, prime the piece with a dark color. You can use the actual color that you intend for the final finish, if you have enough, but in a pinch a primer coat can be white. Sand the primer coat lightly and wipe away the sand grit. Mix a small amount of white latex paint and a drop of red acrylic to get the raspberry color for the background. Continue to add more paint as you mix, until you have enough of a mixture to cover the chair completely. In this case you might use one tube of the acrylic color. (A sponge brush can be used to apply the paint. This can later be cleaned in water and used again for varnishing.) Let the chair dry for a couple of hours. Sand all surfaces very lightly.

The paper doilies come in all sizes and shapes as well as designs. I cut the ones used here to look like snowflakes. In this way

Cut doilies to size.

I was able to cut down an oversized doily so that it would be in proportion to the object. The smaller circles are cut from the centers of the doilies. When cutting, you can do several at a time, because the doilies are stuck together and must be peeled apart anyway. Play around with different arrangements. It took quite a while before I knew that this arrangement would look good on the chair. These die-cut papers are embossed and slightly raised, but when they are glued to the wood surface, they flatten out. This makes covering them with varnish no problem.

When you have the doilies placed the way you think they look best, make a pencil dot on the chair through the hole in the center of each one. This will be your guide for placement once you remove the doilies for gluing. The small circles do not need to be marked, because they can be applied once the larger ones are glued in place. It will be easy to see where they should go.

Pour a small amount of Elmer's Glue-All into a bowl or paper cup. Add to this a few drops of water, so that the glue is easy to spread. Mix this with the same sponge brush used for painting. Start at one corner in the back and work forward. Brush the diluted glue over the section where the first doily will be placed. Carefully lay the doily over the glue. Smoosh more glue over the paper doily so that it is well saturated. Do not rub the glue into the doily, because the paper is quite delicate and might rip. Take a damp sponge and firmly press down on top of the glued doily. Again, do not rub. The doily will become slightly translucent, and the painted

Apply glue to chair.

Place doily in position.

color from underneath will show through, softening the whiteness of the paper.

Continue to place each cut-out doily in this way until the entire surface is covered. Don't be afraid to apply plenty of glue; it will dry clear. When the larger pieces are in place, add the small cutouts in between. Cut several in half and place them around the seat edges. Three large doily snowflakes are used for the top back rung; smaller ones are used for the second back rung. Let the glue dry for about half an hour.

Saturate doily with glue.

You will probably want to put high-gloss varnish on this object, or on any similar piece of furniture that will get a lot of use. The high-gloss finish will give it a hard, protective coating as well as a shiny, wet look. While almost any indoor wood varnish is fine to use, polyurethane varnish is best for this project.

Pour a small pool of varnish in the center of the seat so that the varnish will not drip and run over the sides. Working from the center, use the sponge brush to draw the varnish out toward the sides. Cover the rest of the chair without redipping the brush into the can of varnish. The sponge brush holds quite a bit of varnish, and you will achieve a smooth, drip-free surface if you don't overload it. If it seems difficult to *brush* over the doilies, dab the varnish on this area. After the first coat it will be easy to apply the second and third coats. Brush the varnish over the underside of the rungs and front area in order to seal out moisture.

Each coat of varnish will take twenty-four hours to dry thoroughly. After each coat, leave the piece in an out-of-the-way place until the next day. Never varnish over a tacky finish.

Tamp doily down gently.

Although three coats of varnish are the minimum required to sufficiently cover the design, I prefer and recommend at least five coats in order to create a smooth surface. It is best when you can run your hand over the chair and not feel the raised areas of the design.

After five coats, you can sand lightly. Do not apply pressure, or you will run the risk of sanding away parts of the paper doilies. The sanding should be done with the finest grade of sandpaper, for example, 3M's WetorDry No. 400. This will remove tiny particles that have dried in the varnish and caused the surface to become rough. A rub-down with very fine steel wool will further smooth the surface. Follow this with a coat of clear paste wax such as

Do not disturb other doilies when setting new one in position.

Johnson's Furniture Paste Wax or Butcher's Bowling Alley Paste Wax.

If you have a small table to go with the chairs, consider using the same technique on it. If the table is square, you could use square doilies as place mats. For a small round table, you might find a large round doily to more or less fit over the entire top area. Glue these in place and varnish in the same way. After varnishing, examine the object from various angles to see if any areas have been missed. It is often easy to overlook a spot or two because the varnish is clear.

And there you have it—a very simple technique for creating an unusual design while making the chair totally childproof.

Colors to Sit On

A couple of years ago a fabric printed with a graphic design caught my eye. Large, boldly striped A, B, C letters march across a navy-blue background. I thought it might look good attached to a canvas stretcher and used as a wall decoration in one of my daughters' rooms. I never got around to using it, but I've kept it in the back of my mind as a source of inspiration. Wallpaper or fabric is a good place to look for a design idea. This bold, bright design seemed appropriate for the third chair. You could adapt this design to any color combination that suits your room. It is quite easy to do and the materials needed are few.

A chair can be spruced up by paint alone.

Materials Needed: Primer paint, background paint, paintbrush, masking tape, approximately five tubes of acrylic paints, high-gloss polyurethane varnish or indoor wood varnish, two-inch-wide sponge brush, brush cleaner, fine sandpaper.

Begin by priming and painting the background. If you are matching the paint to fabric, do the mixing in daylight for accuracy. Mixing paint colors can be fun. Acrylic paint can be used straight from the tube, or you can mix it with latex paint. The paint color is quite intense when used straight from the tube. Combining a drop of acrylic with a cup of white latex paint will create a pastel. Combine pigments a little at a time until you bring the color as close as possible to what you are matching. Paint a small section and let it dry before painting the entire object. Sometimes paint will dry darker than when you first apply it.

Use a piece of cardboard or any straight edge to mark off the stripes. Divide the seat area into four sections, as shown. Don't be concerned about transferring the design precisely, as long as it looks right. I've rendered the center stripes here narrower than the end triangles so that the colored areas on each corner would not be too small. Mix each of the colors you'll need. I copied the fabric hues exactly with red, orange, green, and yellow. I've kept the chair design simple and restrained to reflect the design of the fabric. At one point, I wanted to stencil a child's name across the top, alternating the colors for each letter, but the feeling of the fabric is straightforward and contemporary, and this addition would not have been in keeping with the unadorned design. I could, however, imagine repeating this design across a dresser or headboard in a child's room.

54

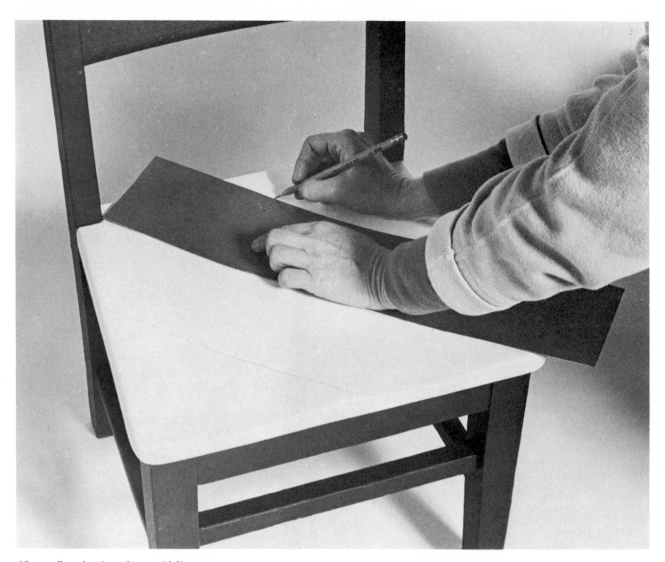

Use cardboard strip to draw guidelines.

Lay a piece of masking tape along the first line. Paint the corner stripe. The tape will ensure a crisp and perfect boundary where the first color ends and the second begins. Let the paint dry before taping over it and painting the next color. The acrylic paint is rubbery and thick and will require only one coat, even mixed with latex.

Coat the entire chair with high-gloss polyurethane or indoor wood varnish for a shiny finish. Let this dry overnight and re-apply. A two-inch-wide sponge brush is best; it should be cleaned between

Remove tape before paint dries.

applications in brush cleaner. (These brushes are not meant to last past one or two jobs, but they are inexpensive and easy to work with.) After three coats of varnish, sand the entire object lightly and varnish once more for added smoothness and extra protection. The fabric used here comes from Fabrications, a delightful fabric store in New York and Boston. Check the "Sources for Supplies" at the back of the book for their mailing addresses. If you have three chairs, you might want to paint all three exactly the same and line them up against a wall, each under a different letter on the fabric.

Mirrored Towel Rack

This lovely converted towel rack was once a headboard that I discovered last summer while taking one of many tours around the island dump. The sea gulls hovered over the garbage while I scrounged among the cleaner refuse. Not all dump yards are accessible, nor do they yield interesting discarded pieces of furniture. However, you might find such an item with recycling potential in your attic, basement, or Goodwill outlet or at yard sales. This headboard was once part of an old-fashioned bed. The legs were still intact, and the wood curved up and away from where the bed was attached. One look and I knew that this could make an interesting piece with a little work on my part.

At home I cleaned it up with detergent and a steel wool pad. Then I sawed off the legs so they were flush with the wood panel and sanded this smooth. While the wood is nicer on the front than the back, the only way I could imagine using this was as a towel holder in the bathroom or kitchen, which meant turning it back to front in order to utilize the curved railing. The large panel area

Some old finishes sand off easily.

suggested the possibility of setting a mirror into it. Other ideas I had were to fill the area with a corkboard for messages or to decorate it with a stenciled design. However, the mirror idea seemed best, so I settled on that. Many objects that seem like discards would be terrific for this kind of project. Consider the back of a chair or a paneled door. A found object, when combined with a good eye for the unusual, can be transformed into a good-looking, unique, inexpensive, and useful item.

Stain before mounting mirror.

Materials Needed: Sandpaper, electric finishing sander or hand sanding block, dark walnut stain, molding strips, razor blade or X-Acto knife, putty knife, contact cement, mirror in desired size, wallpaper border design, Elmer's Glue-All, two-inch-wide paintbrush, high-gloss polyurethane varnish, brush cleaner, very fine steel wool, furniture paste wax.

This bed frame wasn't made of pretty wood, and the old lacquered finish practically fell off when I sanded the piece. I am so addicted to the electric finishing sander that I look for excuses to use it. However, this object could have been as effectively sanded with a hand sanding block. After sanding, I cleaned away the dust to prepare the wood for restaining. This piece could have been painted, but I felt that a dark walnut stain would enhance it and

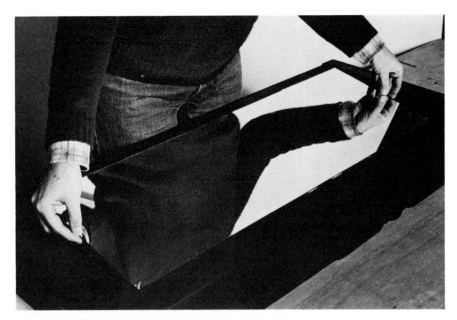

Make contact with one edge first.

Press mirror gently all over.

perhaps make the wood look better than it actually is. This wood, being old with little of the original finish still on it, was very dry. It took three coatings of stain to bring it back to life. The color is not as dark as I would have liked, but the application of varnish will brighten most stained finishes, giving them a high luster.

Measure the area that will contain the mirror. Having a mirror cut to the exact size can be expensive, but if your piece is square or rectangular you might be able to obtain a leftover piece to fit. Glass and mirror shops often have odd pieces left over from other jobs.

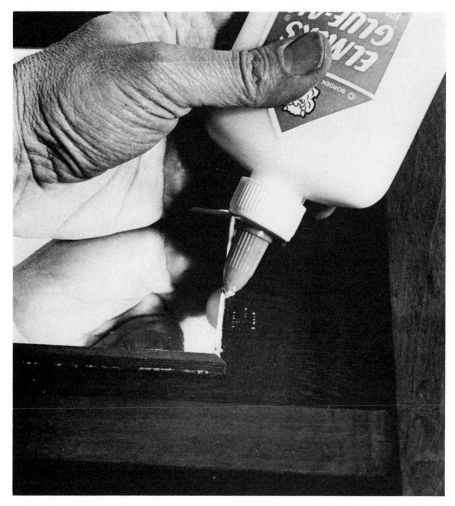

Run line of white glue along edge.

The narrow strips of wood around the mirror give it a finished look. It is difficult to find molding for this purpose. The molding I found in lumberyards was too wide, so I checked with a picture-framing shop. Again I wasn't able to get the right size. The quarter-inch strips used here are the best I could find for this project. They are found in hobby stores and five-and-tens, usually with the balsa wood. They are soft and can be cut with a razor blade or an X-Acto knife. When staining the wood frame, don't forget to stain the strips before mounting them. Cut them so they are mitered at each corner (see photo).

To mount a mirror on a wood surface you will need a putty knife and contact cement. First lay the mirror on the surface and draw a line around it. Remove the mirror and spread a coat of the contact cement over the wood surface to be covered. Spread the contact cement on the back of the mirror as well. Let the cement set

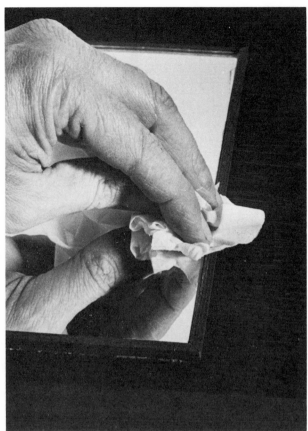

Press molding into position.

Remove excess glue with damp cloth.

according to the directions on the can. Now carefully place the mirror over the sticky area and gently press it down around the edges and in the center. Glue the strips of "molding" around the mirror and adjust them so that the corners butt. These strips will finish off any rough edges on the mirror.

In this case the plywood around the mirror did not look good and needed an attractive finishing touch. A stenciled decoration might have done the trick to distract the eye from the wood, but the area is rather narrow and awkward to work on. The application of a wallpaper border covers the less attractive wood and helps tie the project in with the rest of the decor in the room. The border can easily be attached with Elmer's Glue-All.

A decoupage mirror towel rack.

Finally, the entire piece, excluding the mirror, is given a coat of high-gloss polyurethane varnish. Leave this to dry thoroughly for twenty-four hours before rubbing the surface lightly with very fine steel wool. Apply furniture paste wax to protect the wood and buff with a soft cloth.

Obviously you cannot duplicate this project exactly, but if you find an interesting fragment of an old piece of furniture, this example might encourage you to make something out of it that will be useful to you. Odd pieces of wood sometimes make excellent frames for pictures or custom-cut mirrors. Remember that wallpaper and fabric can be used to disguise unsightly surfaces on well-shaped pieces.

Table Greenery

Once the windowsills are filled with plants, it's sometimes hard to find a way to display plants that don't fit on the sills. When my plants began to spill over onto the floor, I found that they could be arranged effectively on small stands or an occasional table, which enabled me to group them and vary their heights. Look at a small step stool or outgrown child's chair with this in mind. Even a little desk can offer an unusual surface for displaying various plants.

This little table was literally on its last legs. Wobbly and poorly painted, it desperately needed repair. Not too terrific as a table, it has a great deal of appeal as a plant stand. It is small and low and has a rectangular top. Unobtrusive in size and shape, it makes a good support without drawing attention away from any plants that might be placed on top.

Apply design freehand with rubber cement.

The technique I used to decorate this table is so simple that a child might enjoy helping. The design is executed in freehand with paint and rubber cement, and you don't have to be able to draw a straight line. A good design idea is what makes this idea work, and finding a good design idea should never be a problem. Look around you. Such natural forms as ferns, leaves, flowers, and petals are good motifs to start with. Perhaps a wallpaper or fabric or dinnerware pattern can be copied. I took the design for this table from the Wall-Tex vinyl wallcovering in the room where the table will be placed. It is an abstract pattern in brilliant green, which seems appropriate as a background for plants.

Materials Needed: One tube of silver acrylic paint, one tube of bright green acrylic paint, water, sponge brush, sandpaper, primer or latex paint, rubber cement, rubber cement thinner, jar or paper plate, soft clean cloth, rubber-cement pickup, narrow tapered brush, high-gloss or satin polyurethane varnish, brush cleaner, furniture paste wax.

Brush glaze on and wipe it off.

Sand the entire object before painting. Give the table a primer coat of white latex paint. Let this dry. Sand the surface lightly to create a smooth area for the acrylic paint. The background color used here is silver acrylic, which I thinned with water so it would go on more easily. Apply one coat of the silver paint with a sponge brush. After use, clean the brush in warm water. The paint will dry quickly. If your table needs a second coat of paint, sand lightly before applying more paint.

Dip the tapered brush into the can of rubber cement and paint your design on the table. If you feel unsure about doing this freehand, first trace and transfer a design onto the surface. The point here, however, is that the look be random and carefree. The technique is best achieved when there is no real planning involved. This is the perfect crafting style for those who do not like doing exacting work. There is no way to miss with this project. It took ten minutes to do. Simply paint the pattern on with the rubber cement. It won't and shouldn't be perfect.

The rubber cement will dry quickly. Check the table in a well-lighted area to make sure the rubber cement has "taken" in all sections; since it is transparent, it's often difficult to see where you may have failed to apply it. Clean the brush with rubber cement thinner when you are through.

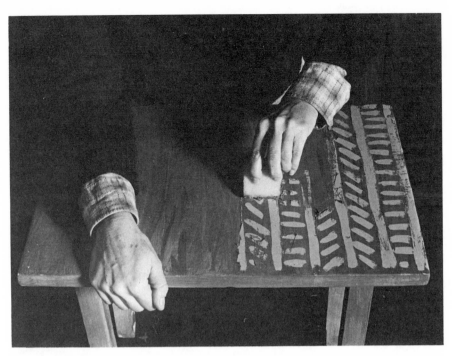

Rubber cement pickup reveals design.

Next, thin the bright green acrylic paint with water by squirting about a tablespoonful of paint into a jar or onto a paper plate and adding enough water to create a thin consistency. Paint the entire table with the solution right over the silver and rubber cement design. You can apply it any which way, and if it streaks it will look fine. Make irregular patterns by wiping the paint with a clean, soft cloth as you go along, but don't wipe away too much paint. Re-apply where necessary, but remember, the paint shouldn't be too thick. It may even bead up and separate over the rubber cement, which is all right. Let the paint dry completely.

Now that your table looks a mess and you are sure that all the preparatory work was in vain, you are in for a surprise. The rubber-cement pickup is a small, inexpensive, but extremely useful item. It looks like a flat, hard eraser. Pull it over the painted surface, removing all the rubber cement as you go. As the pickup pulls the rubber cement away, the base color—in this case, silver—will be revealed. Don't worry if the design is crude. This is the nature of the craft. It is so easy that you'll be inspired to decorate other items this way. Rub your fingers over the surface to be sure all particles of paint and rubber cement are removed. Your finger is a good substitute for the rubber-cement pickup in the event that you are unable to find the pickup. This method simply requires more elbow grease or, in this case, finger grease.

You can leave the piece as is or give it a protective coating of varnish. The latter is a good idea if you will be using it to hold plants, because the varnish will protect it against moisture. For a shiny, contemporary look, use high-gloss polyurethane wood var-

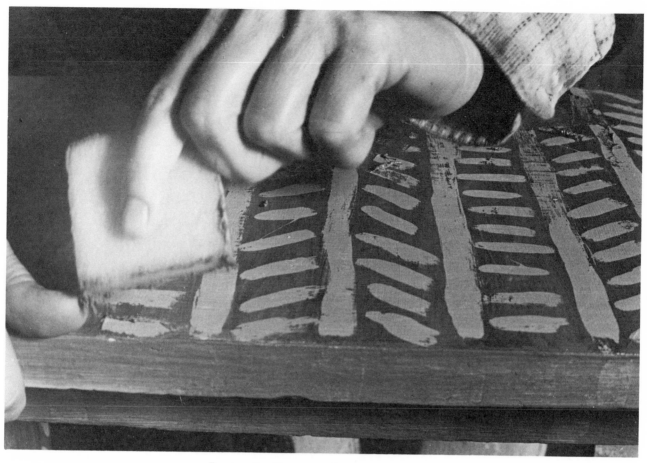

Remove all rubber cement for smooth surface.

nish. If you would prefer a subtle, soft glow, use satin-finish varnish. You can use the same sponge brush used for painting, after it has been cleaned. (Once the brush has been used for varnish, however, you cannot use it for water-base paint again.) Apply a thin coat of varnish to the entire surface, including the underneath. This will seal the wood and retard warping. Let the varnish dry overnight and then apply a second coat. If, when dry, the varnished table feels bumpy, sand it lightly with a very fine grade of sandpaper. Polish the top with furniture paste wax and arrange your plants on it.

Design possibilities for this technique are limitless. You might want to use it for outdoor furniture as well. Try simple illustrations—perhaps coloring book designs—on children's furniture. You can use more than two colors, and more complicated designs as well. To add a third color, re-apply the rubber cement and put another color on in the same way. The rubber-cement technique is also useful if you have an old piece that needs repainting but has a painted design worth preserving. Carefully paint the existing design with rubber cement. Then paint the entire chair as you would normally. When the paint dries, remove the rubber cement and the original design will be intact.

New Life for an Old Chair

A sturdy, well-proportioned wooden dining-room or kitchen chair with an upholstered seat is probably the easiest kind of project to spruce up. It is a cinch to remove the seat from the chair rails and redo it. You can match the new seat cover to fabric you've already used in a room, or you can choose new fabric that can be changed often. You needn't buy expensive fabric to create an unusual effect. I found quite an elegant remnant for $1.25 in the five-and-ten; the background color is wine and the flowers are cream color. This dictated the colors for the wooden chair frame. The frame was originally aqua blue and simply needed a light sanding before receiving a coat of the cream color that matches the flowers in the pattern. The carved area in the back was unattractive before the new paint job. With a tapered artist's brush, the inner surfaces were carefully given a contrasting wine color to match the fabric. This is a nice touch and brings out the design.

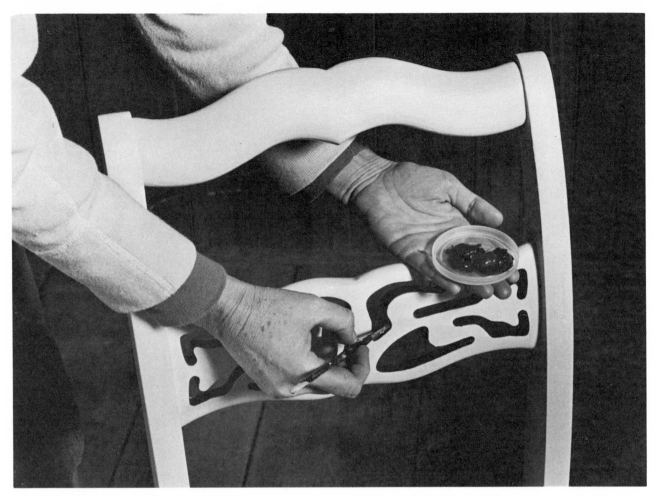

Use small brush to paint details.

The padding under the old fabric seemed to be intact, but if the padding in your seat has deteriorated slightly, you can augment it easily.

Materials Needed: A half yard of fabric per seat (this should cover most seat areas), screwdriver, tack or staple remover, cotton batting (or foam rubber or polyfoam) if seat needs padding, scissors, paint, two-inch brush, tapered artist's brush for detail work if necessary, indoor wood varnish (optional), brush cleaner.

Turn the chair upside down and unscrew the screw from each corner of the underside of the seat. This will release the seat so that you can remove the old covering. Upholstery tacks or staples holding the fabric to the seat board must also be removed. If the old stuffing is no longer full enough to cushion the chair, you can fill in with extra batting or make a new cushion with 1½- to 2-inch-thick foam rubber or polyfoam. Lay the chair seat on the foam and cut

Trim fabric to include overlap.

around it with a sharp knife or scissors. Or trace around the perimeter of the seat frame to make a paper pattern to cut the foam cushion from.

Use the chair seat as a template to cut the covering fabric. Again, if you want to make a paper pattern, do so. However, the chair seat should be sufficient and save this extra step. Cut the fabric at least 1½ inches larger all around than the seat size to allow for turning it under and tacking it. When the fabric is turned to the underside, it should not cover the screw holes at each corner.

Lay the fabric down wrong-side up. Place the seat on the fabric with the padding down. Start in the center of one side and turn the edge under. Pull it slightly taut and staple to the underside of the chair seat. If you don't have a staple gun use ⅜- or ½-inch tacks. Do this on the opposite side so that the fabric is smooth and taut. Secure the fabric at the back and front of the chair as well. Cut off the

Stretch and staple fabric taut.

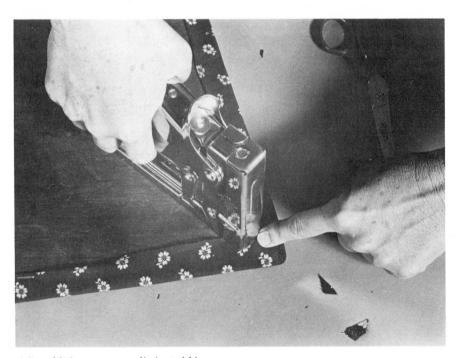

Adjust fabric at corner to eliminate folds.

corners diagonally to make it easier to fold and tuck this area without bunching. Work with the corners until the fabric is tight and smooth before securing with staples or tacks.

Turn the newly covered seat over and place it on the chair frame to be sure it will fit in place. Now turn the chair upside down again, this time with the chair seat in place. Drop the screws back into the original holes and tighten. You can see how easy it would be to

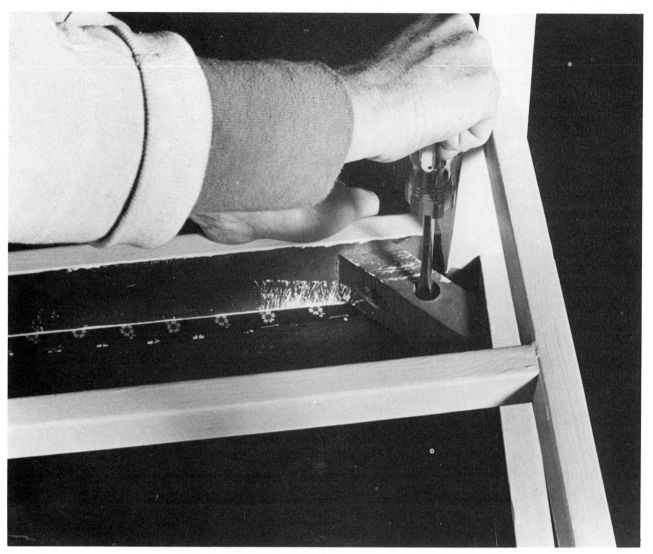

Screw seat into chair frame.

replace the coverings again, and since each chair doesn't require much fabric, you can change the coverings as often as you like.

To protect the new painted or stained finish, apply a thin coat of indoor wood varnish over the wooden frame. Let it dry thoroughly before using the chair.

A tip: When buying the fabric to re-cover dining-room or kitchen chairs, why not purchase some extra fabric to make matching place mats?

Decoupage Sideboard

One of the editors at *House and Garden* magazine posed a problem that I enjoyed solving. In her summer house she had an old sideboard that was chipped, warped, and scratched. It had been in her basement for quite a while, and the dampness had penetrated the wood. She wanted to have it revived, if possible, for inclusion in an article about what to do with old furniture, and then for installing in an upstairs hallway. She thought the piece would be perfect for holding extra blankets and linens for the guest room. The people at the magazine suggested a traditional design with an Oriental flavor. Indeed a challenge! I decided to use the technique of decoupage for this project.

Everyone has grown up with the skills needed for decoupage. If you can cut, paint, and paste you can follow these easy step-by-step directions. Decoupage means applied cutouts, and the process, which originated in France during the eighteenth century, involves decorating with paper cutouts. In other words, there is no painting involved in the artwork, and anything that has been printed is a potential design element.

Look through some illustrated books to find delicate flowers, leaves, or grasses that might work well against the background color you've chosen. The Golden Nature Guide series of paperback field guides on such subjects as trees, shells, and butterflies has lots of illustrations good for decoupage. Magazines are readily available, but the paper is too thin and the print from the other side shows through when varnished. For this project, to evoke an Oriental feeling I chose delicate butterflies and thin blades of grass to arrange on the red background, and here and there I added a few flower blossoms. The colors are subtle, mostly white, pale yellow, and light green.

Strip old finish.

Materials Needed: One can all-purpose paint remover (or finishing sander) if your piece is in poor condition and needs to be stripped, scraper or putty knife, fine steel wool, two sponge brushes, quart can of white latex paint, large tube of red acrylic paint, cut-out paper designs, cuticle scissors, Elmer's Glue-All, sponge, high-gloss polyurethane varnish, brush cleaner, two pieces of sandpaper (fine and very fine), antiquing mix (optional), clear furniture paste wax.

If the piece of furniture you're working on has a painted finish, you can remove it with an all-purpose paint remover such as Strypeeze, which is available in all hardware stores. If there is a

Completely stripped piece.

commercial stripper in your area, consider saving your labor and having it done professionally. However, if the painted finish is not badly damaged, you can sand the surfaces smooth with an electric finishing sander to prepare it for painting.

Begin with a primer coat of paint in the color you've chosen for the piece. To duplicate the background color of my buffet, mix Grumbacher red acrylic paint with the white latex wall paint until you obtain a cherry-red shade. You will need to apply two coats of a dark-colored paint like this one, in addition to the primer coat; for a pastel-colored background you may need three extra coats. Spray painting over the base coat can make the job easier, but the range of colors available may not offer exactly what you want. When the last coat is completely dry, sand the painted surface lightly using fine sandpaper.

Cut out the paper designs with cuticle scissors. Do this carefully so that you trim away all superfluous paper without cutting jagged edges around the illustrations. (When selecting your designs, keep

Apply paint smoothly.

in mind that you will be cutting them out. You might want to avoid a very lacy, intricate design that would be difficult to cut.)

Experiment with different design arrangements before gluing. Stand back and look critically at the arrangement. Don't be afraid to toss out parts of designs that don't seem right or to add to them here and there. For this cabinet, I concentrated the designs near the edges and around the knobs. All the designs are arranged on the front, leaving the top clear. More cutouts could have been extended up onto the top. This is a matter of preference. You'll know when your piece has enough decoration for your taste.

When you are happy with the way it looks, lift one piece at a time and coat the back with Elmer's Glue-All. Don't overload, but

Cut out prints with cuticle scissors.

be sure you have coated the paper, especially on the edges. Press the piece in its place on the surface. Remove excess glue with a damp sponge.

When you've finished applying the cutouts, coat the entire surface with varnish. For this piece I used high-gloss polyurethane varnish. The many coats of varnish will give the piece a highly lacquered appearance and the decorations will be embedded beneath the surface. For best results, apply the varnish on a dry day. Start in the center of the top and work toward the edges. It is best to apply thin coats rather than float a thick coating over the surface. Allow each coat twenty-four hours to dry thoroughly before applying subsequent coats. This is the secret of a lasting and beautiful

Apply antiquing glaze.

finish. After the third coat, sand very lightly before applying the next coat. Use WetorDry No. 400 sandpaper and moisten it slightly each time you sand. Wipe away sand grit with a soft, clean cloth.

The more coats of varnish you use, the smoother the finish. Altogether you will apply from five to ten coats of varnish. If you'd like a slightly raised effect, which means that you can feel the design when you run your hand over the surface, fewer coats are required. For an extra-smooth surface, rub lightly over the piece with fine steel wool.

If you would like to add a bit of "antique" character to the piece, apply an antiquing mixture sparingly. An earth color, such as raw umber, is best. Dab a little in the corners around the hinges and knobs and blend it with a clean cloth. Lift the cloth gradually as you wipe toward the center to blend the color. If you are working on curved or grooved areas, leave the excess antiquing in the crevices to imitate the collection of grime and aging. Let this dry, then coat with varnish and sand with the WetorDry No. 400 sandpaper for a final finish. Polish with clear furniture paste wax and buff with a soft cloth.

Antiquing prior to final coat of varnish.

Orange-Section Table

This funky table was found in two pieces in a friend's attic. The base rested in a corner, and the very badly warped top lay under some baby crib mattresses. The veneer was chipped and bubbled and more off the piece than on. In sum, the table verged on being ready for the junk heap. But its size and shape were too good to pass up, so I gave it a complete overhaul that took more than a week. Now that it's finished, you can see it was worth the time and effort.

The top wouldn't fit back onto the base because of the warping. Warping is easily corrected. Check "Tips on Repairing and Preparing" to find out how to repair general warping. Since this tabletop was too large to set on a radiator, and the weather hadn't been good enough to let it bask in the sun, a new approach was necessary. I placed the tabletop concave side up on top of the warm furnace, where it rested for several days. This removed some of the warping. Next, I poured boiling water onto the concave area and returned the top to its place on the warm furnace. After twenty-four hours, the top began to appear somewhat normal. One more day, spent standing on the floor while leaning against the radiator, did it. There is still a slight curve, but it is not noticeable unless you study it.

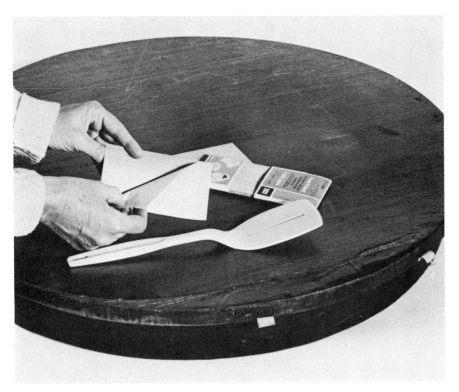

Peel sticky-backed sandpaper.

Stick sandpaper to spatula.

Next, the loose and decaying veneer had to be fixed. I removed the old glue from the surfaces under the veneer that had lifted away by improvising the following technique. I wrapped a piece of

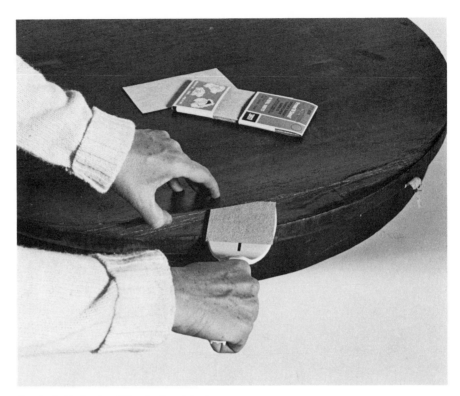

Sand off old glue by sliding back and forth.

Re-glue surface and weight down until dry.

sticky-backed Press 'N Sand sandpaper around the end of a cooking spatula, wet it slightly, and slid it under the lifted veneer, sanding back and forth. After this I applied Elmer's Carpenter's Wood Glue to the table surface and the underside of the lifting veneer and clamped and weighted down the repair with heavy books. Parts of the base were repaired in the same way. The chipped veneer was removed in parts, sanded here and there, and patched with wood filler. (For how-to details, refer to "Tips on Repairing and Preparing.") I left everything to dry overnight before sanding smooth. The piece was then wiped with a dry cloth and alcohol to remove old wax and dirt.

Clamp veneer wherever possible.

Materials Needed: Press 'N Sand sandpaper, Elmer's Carpenter's Wood Glue, sandpaper, wood filler, alcohol, brown and orange and yellow acrylic paints, white latex paint, two-inch paintbrush, tapered artist's brush, scissors, stencil paper and stencil brush (optional), protractor or 45-degree triangle, varnish, brush cleaner.

The top section of the table is painted to look like the cross section of an orange, and the base is painted dark brown to emphasize the top. Begin with a base coat; brown is used here for the base and white for the top. When the primer coat is dry, apply another coat of brown to the base and white to the rim of the top. If you have a round table, you can re-create this design in the following way. Find the center. Use the protractor or 45-degree triangle to divide the circle into eight equal pie-shaped parts. Next, mix the paints. I used Liquitex Indo-Orange red (every acrylic paint company makes a bright orange color, and each goes by a different name) mixed with white to create a soft orange color. If you use it right from the tube, the color will be too harsh. Paint the orange triangles, rounding off each section and leaving a border unpainted to represent the rind. Save the paint for touch-ups. I find that mixing paint in a paper cup is convenient; if you have to put it aside in the middle of painting, just add a few drops of water to the paint to keep it from drying out.

Next, mix a drop or two of yellow acrylic paint with the white paint to create a very pale yellow. This provides a nice contrast to the dark base and the bright orange. Paint the outer rim and

Use acrylic paints to apply design.

dividing lines between each orange section. Save the pale yellow so that you can refine your work, going back and forth between the orange and yellow colors.

Finally, paint pits onto the orange sections here and there. This can be done with the white paint, which when dry will have a faint orange cast from the orange paint's showing through. If you feel confident, this can be done freehand. However, to make the pits uniform you can stencil them on. Cut a teardrop shape from stencil paper. Using a stencil brush, tap paint over the cut-out area.

Now paint the rim around the edge of the tabletop to look like the outer part of the orange. It needn't be absolutely true to the color of orange rind. Mix brown and orange acrylic paint until you have a pleasing color that is lighter than the base and darker than the orange sections. When dry, varnish the entire project to protect your artwork.

You can have a lot of fun doing a project like this, where mixing, matching, and contrasting paint colors are required. Concentrate on finding a color combination that is pretty. The colors don't have to duplicate those of the object you're representing. Pale colors are quite elegant, and when the right ones are used together the effect is arresting.

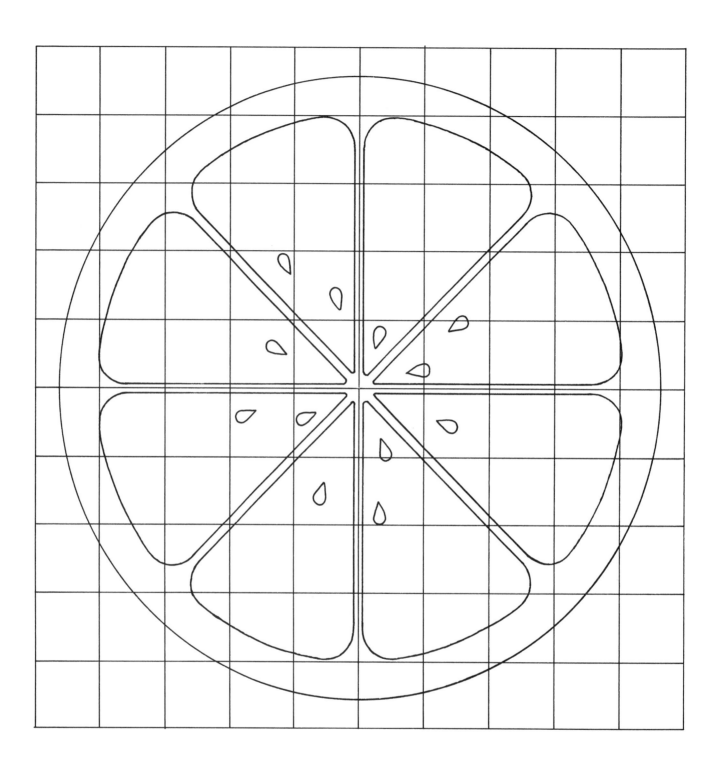

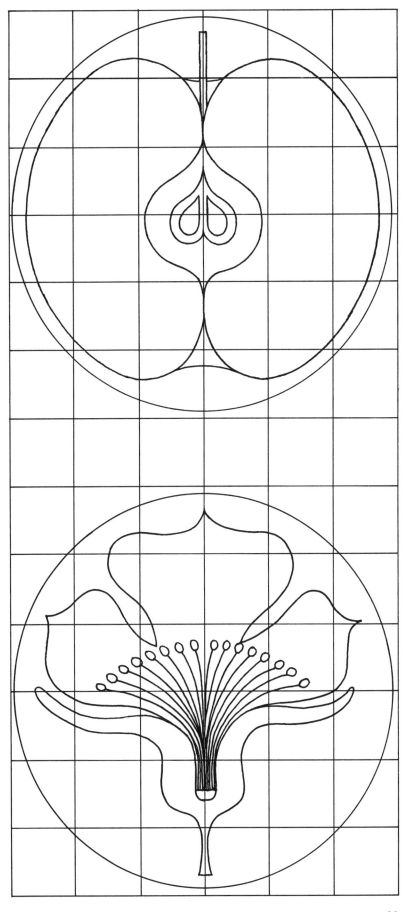

Caned Chairs

Perhaps you've relegated a chair to the attic because the seat has a hole in it and you haven't the faintest idea of how to repair it. Because the wooden frame is so nice, you can't discard the chair completely. The most common item to be found in junk shops for almost any price seems to be the damaged chair. The variety of styles and sizes available arouses my enthusiasm, because it isn't hard to visualize a place for this item at home. Everyone can use an extra chair or two from time to time. Many of the damaged chairs seem to have been caned originally, and, surprisingly, it is not difficult to repair a seat with this crafting technique. Often this is a wonderful solution for salvaging an otherwise perfectly good, delicate wooden chair.

I had never tried caning, but my neighbor Gloria DuBock is the local expert. Her house abounds with chairs of every description, and what began as a hobby has blossomed into a business. One night a week she gives a course in caning, and she finally convinced me to take it. (I was presented with a darling bedroom chair that had a broken caned seat to ensure that I would attend the classes.) Gloria says that when you know how to cane, the skill opens up possibilities for all sorts of home furnishing projects that would otherwise not be feasible.

There are several methods for reseating a chair. The two that we are concerned with here are reseating with cane webbing or pressed cane and handweaving a new cane seat. The cane webbing or pressed cane can be used to reseat a chair that has a groove in the seat frame, which indicates that the chair was originally caned in this way. Most old chairs that were hand caned have holes around the seat frame into which the cane strips are fed. (If you would like to cane a new chair, holes for the cane must be drilled around the perimeter of the seat frame. Make them $3/16$ inch in diameter and space them $5/8$ inch apart.)

Thin strips of reed (spline) are used to hold the cane webbing in place. This is the method I used for my chair, and while everyone else in the class was handweaving week after week, my chair was finished in one evening. My classmates referred to my project as the "pre-fab job," having adopted the view of all craft purists rather quickly. However, web caning is a fast and easy way to repair a chair if you don't want to take the time to do the handwoven process.

Web Caning

To begin my project, I had the chair stripped of its finish. (I started to do this by hand, but by the time I got to the carved areas and spindles I gave up and took it to a commercial stripping outfit.) The old torn seat was then cut away so that only the pieces around the edges that had originally been glued to the frame were left. If you are working on a similar project, you will want to prepare the entire chair by cleaning it before proceeding with the caning.

Materials Needed for Web Caning: Chair with groove in seat frame, about five wedges, rubber mallet or hammer, screwdriver or chisel to remove old spline, cane webbing (bought by the running foot), cuticle scissors, Elmer's Glue-All or Elmer's Carpenter's Wood Glue, spline, X-Acto knife or utility blade (if needed), sponge, indoor wood varnish, brush cleaner. You can find materials for caning in hobby shops or you can obtain them by mail order (see "Sources for Supplies" at the back of the book). These materials are inexpensive, making this a practical as well as a handsome way to repair a chair.

Use wedges to secure cane after cutting.

several times, making sure that the webbing is securely in place. Using small sewing or cuticle scissors, cut the excess webbing away. When cutting, clip the webbing down below the surface of the top of the seat so that it doesn't show. If any webbing lifts out of the groove while you are doing this, place one of the wedges in this spot and hammer it back in.

If the spline is stiff and unpliable, you will have to soak it in hot water just as you did the webbing. When it is ready to be inserted into the groove, squirt plenty of glue in the groove all around. Elmer's Glue-All or Elmer's Carpenter's Wood Glue is good for this.

Hammer spline into groove.

Cut the ends of the spline on the diagonal so they are mitered and are long enough to overlap slightly. Since my chair seat had rounded corners, I used one piece of spline; if you are working on a rectangular chair seat, the spline should be cut in four pieces the lengths of the sides and mitered and joined at each corner. When the spline dries, it will shrink a little bit.

For a seat with rounded corners, lay one end of the spline at the center back and press it into the groove. Using a rubber mallet or hammer on top of a wedge, force the spline into the groove, all the way around the seat. If you are using a hammer, pad it so you don't split or flatten the spline, which is rather soft. If, when you reach the end, there is too much spline left over, you can cut it to fit. This can be done with an X-Acto knife or utility blade. Clean away any excess glue with a sponge and let the chair dry overnight.

100

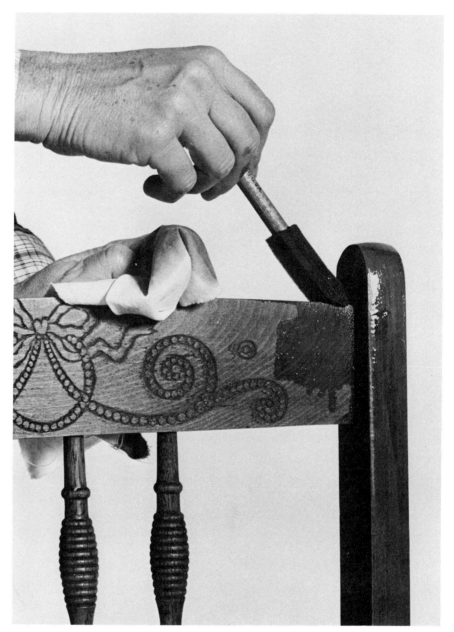

Stain chair frame.

If you're leaving the chair natural, you might want to oil the seat, spline, and frame to bring out the luster of the wood. If you would like to stain the chair, choose the color from samples provided at the hardware store. MinWax wood-penetrating stain comes in a wide variety of colors and is easy to apply. The cane can be stained to match the rest of the wood. In either case, coat the entire piece with wood varnish to protect the finish and to give it a rich, polished appearance.

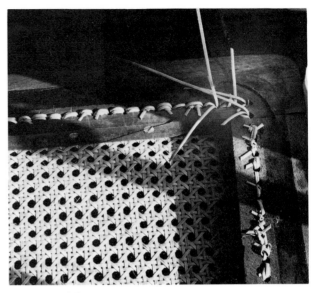

Close-up of Grail Kearney's chair.   *Underside of chair seat.*

Hand Caning

If your chair requires caning done by hand, begin by cleaning out the existing holes. Sometimes these holes have been ruptured and are no longer well defined. In this case, you will have to do some patching with wood filler. Furthermore, the seat area of the chair must be sturdy or you won't have a chair worth the time and effort you put into it. Check to see if the legs must first be glued to the seat to strengthen it. Often you need to screw a piece of wood into the inside back of the open seat area to create a sturdy frame. These are minor repairs.

Materials for Hand Caning: Natural cane strips (in the desired width), warm water, five pegs for hand caning (available where cane is sold), binder cane, sandpaper, indoor wood varnish or stain or oil.

The natural cane can be purchased where basket material is sold, from mail-order sources, and occasionally from an up-holsterer. You will cut strips from the length of cane ordered. It will cost approximately $1.50 for enough cane to finish one chair. The cane strips come in several widths, but if you are a beginner, start with the easiest and most common, which is a medium width.

Step One: Soak the cane in warm water for about five minutes to make it pliable. Find the center holes at the front and back of the seat. Weave a length of the cane down through the back center hole so that about three or four inches hangs down below the seat. Secure this with a peg. (Pegs specially made for this purpose are available where cane is sold, but one of the men in my class found that old wooden golf tees also worked well for this purpose.) Bring the long end of the cane strand to the front center hole, weave it

Cane chair crafted by Grail Kearney.

through to the underside, and insert another peg. Bring the cane up through the hole directly next to the front center hole and pull it to the back and down through the back hole directly opposite. Bring the cane up through the hole next to it at the back and bring it across to the opposite front hole. Repeat this back and forth until the seat area is covered and all front and back holes, except for the corner holes, are filled. Fill up the right side and then repeat this process on the left side of the seat.

Step Two: Insert a strand of cane into the right back corner and secure it with a peg. Pull this strand across the weaving to the left back corner, insert, and secure with another peg. Thread the cane up through the hole directly in front of this and pull it across to the opposite hole on the right side. Repeat this pattern until you have created a checkerboard pattern across the seat.

Step Three: Begin again by starting in the back center and repeating Step One. In this way you will have sandwiched the

Gloria Du Bock replacing seat on old chair.

strands from Step Two between the first and third weavings. The cane strands for this step are woven into the same holes as in Step One. When this is complete, fasten all the end strands under the seat by tying one to the other in secure knots. As the cane dries, the knots will tighten.

Step Four: For this step, you use the same holes as for Step Two. Begin at the right back corner and thread the cane through the corner hole, securing with a peg. Weave the strand of cane under and over the layer woven in Step One. The strands that go under are always on the right, while the "over" strand is to the left. Continue to fill in the seat until you reach the front. Wet the cane again if it becomes dry and difficult to work with; this will keep it from splitting. If you have to put your work aside before you are finished weaving, place a wet towel over the area to keep it moist.

Step Five: Now for the diagonal weaving. Begin at the back right corner and thread the strand through the left front corner, weaving the cane under the strands that run from side to side and over those going from front to back. The weaving moves from across the widest part of the seat to the right front corner, creating a triangle. Weave the first triangle of the seat, keeping the strand in a straight diagonal

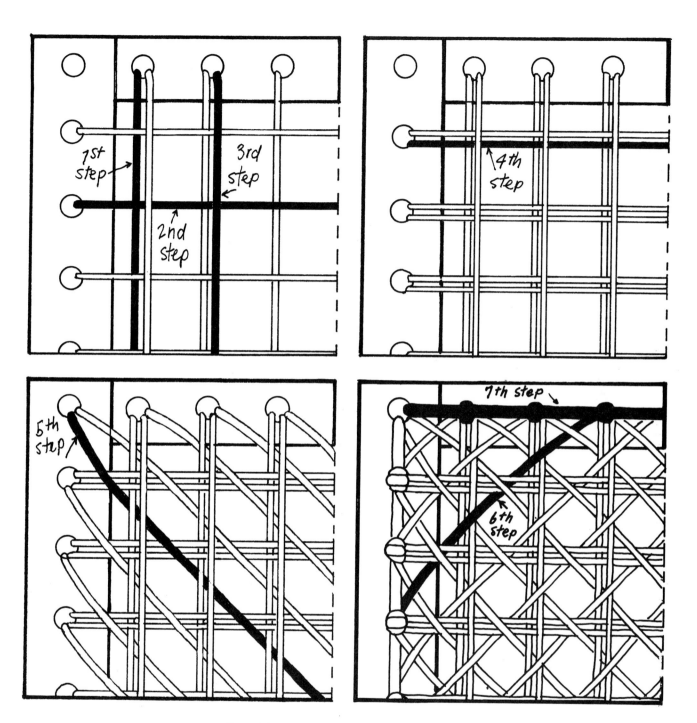

line. If your seat is square, you will end up with two strands in each corner hole.

Step Six: To weave the next triangular half, begin with a strand in the right back corner as before. This means that there will be two strands in this corner. This time, however, your destination is the back left corner, the corner opposite the destination in Step Five. Complete this portion of the seat in the way you wove the first triangle in Step Five.

Step Seven: Starting at the back left corner hole, bring your strand under the strands running from back to front and over those

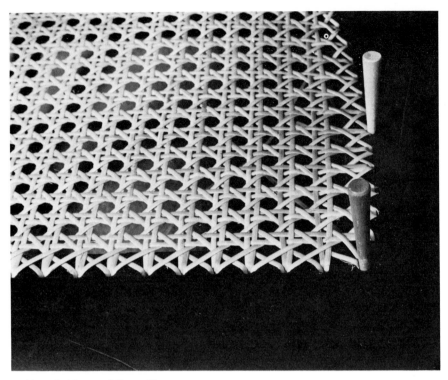

Golf tees hold cane while working.

running from side to side. Then repeat the diagonal weave of the last two steps to form two new triangles. The strands in these triangles run perpendicular to those in the original triangles. Again, two strands will be fed into the corner hole. With this step you will have made a hexagonal hole pattern for the caning.

Step Eight: A piece of binder cane is used to finish the edges. The binder cane should be wide enough to cover the holes. Place one end of the binder into the right corner hole and secure it with a peg. Lay it down across the back chair holes. Tie a knot in one end of a fresh strand of weaving cane and weave the other end up through the corner hole right next to the binder hole. Bring it over the binder and down through the same hole, forming a loop over the binder. In this way you will secure the binder and finish off the back of the chair. Continue to do this all the way around the seat frame, pulling tightly to secure the binder.

Step Nine: To finish off the corners, push the ends of the binder down through the hole. Place a wooden peg into each hole and cut it off so that it is even with the chair. Sand it smooth. A pencil might substitute for a peg here. Shove the pointed end into the hole so that it is tight. Trim it with a sharp implement (such as a utility saw or penknife) and sand it even with the chair seat. The pencil stub will not be obvious when it is stained with the rest of the wood frame.

Step Ten: Stain, oil, or varnish the chair, the underside as well as the top. If you like, the natural color of the cane can be stained to match the wood.

Refurbished footstool.

Child's chair with rush seat by Gloria DuBock.

These instructions are for the most basic caning techniques and a square-seated chair. However, you are likely to find chairs whose seats are not perfectly square. In those cases, I suggest you refer to one of the many books available that give instructions for different caning patterns. The mail-order caning supply source I've listed in the "Sources for Supplies," the Perkins Company, includes with your order a very basic step-by-step diagram for caning round and square seats.

Sponge-Glazed Night Table

A fantasy finish created by applying a glaze with a sponge is the perfect technique for updating the look of an old table. This night table had peeling veneer and two or three coats of paint on it, but the lines are pretty and the size is appealing, making it worth the effort of making over. This slapdash painting can be attractive on any outmoded or distressed furniture that might be used in a child's room, entryway, or family room. I would not recommend it for fine furniture, because it is intended to be fanciful.

Since the veneer was half on and half off, removing it made more sense than repairing it. This didn't seem like a big job until I started. Actually, the rest of the veneer was quite attached and resisted my prying. However, with very hot water, some vinegar, and a chisel I managed to remove the veneer without chipping the surface underneath too badly. (See section on removing veneer in "Tips on Repairing and Preparing.") In some areas where it was especially difficult to remove, I used a wood plane. Next, I filled any scratches and gouges with wood filler, which I left to dry overnight before I sanded the surface smooth.

Use vinegar to loosen the glue.

Plane the last vestiges of veneer.

Fill scratches with wood filler.

Sand surface smooth.

Paint on a new finish.

To apply this finish, first give your piece a base coat of white enamel paint. The fantasy-glaze finish is achieved by sponging a glaze over the entire piece and then making swirls and imprints in the glaze with rags or your fingers. Almost anything goes, and you can feel free to experiment as you go along.

Materials Needed: Flat white enamel paint, small bottle of Japan color or a tube of oil paint, turpentine, boiled linseed oil, two-inch brush, Japan drier, clear varnish, sponges cut in small pieces, stencil brush or paintbrush (optional), high-gloss polyurethane varnish. These materials are available in art supply stores.

To make the glaze, put approximately one ounce of turpentine in a glass jar. Add half as much boiled linseed oil, about one teaspoonful of color, and a drop of drier. Mix everything together well. The solution will be thin and semi-transparent. Try it out on a

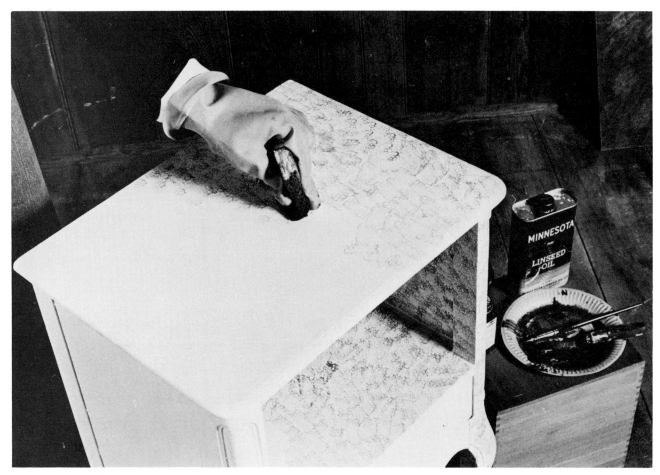

Apply fantasy finish.

scrap piece of board or on an area of the piece that is not too prominent. Experiment until you get the effect that is most pleasing.

Using a small dry sponge to apply the glaze, dip the sponge into the color and lightly blot it on a clean cloth to get rid of some of the excess moisture. Then simply dab the color onto the furniture. Take care not to cover an area with too much color. Do one small area at a time rather than working here and there at random. This will give you a chance to study the effect before covering the entire piece. If you don't like the results in one area you can wipe it away and begin again. Because the glaze takes twenty-four hours to dry, you can play around with it before deciding on your final patterns. Try using a stipple brush or smooshing a paintbrush onto the surface to create other effects. Use your fingers to create swirls in the glaze. You can wipe, dab, run, or even spatter the color with a toothbrush onto the surface. For the night table, I used the sponge to create an overall regular pattern of dabs.

Let the piece dry for twenty-four hours. You might want to decorate accessories to match, employing the same technique. I did a wooden letter holder that, along with similar items, can be found in craft shops. It is made of wood and was first sanded, then given a

Experiment with techniques for creating fantasy finish.

base coat of white. Then I applied the color glaze with a stipple brush to give it texture. Next I made swirls in the glazed finish with my fingers. I experimented on the wooden wastebasket, and each side has a different fantasy pattern. The little basket was spray painted with white enamel, then the glaze was dabbed on with an artist's brush so that it hit the raised areas.

When your glazed furniture dries, apply a coat of clear high-gloss polyurethane varnish to all exposed areas. This protects the finish and gives everything a shiny glow.

Kitchen Chair Comes Alive

Kitchen chairs that can be picked up for very little money are easy to find. Almost everyone has a chair around the house that could use a coat of paint, although we never seem to get around to applying it. I had so much fun working on these chairs that I wanted to do several in order to have one for each member of my family.

Actually, I stared at this chair for a long time before inspiration hit. I was looking for a technique that would be fun, inexpensive, and a little different from anything else I'd done. The first idea I came up with employed the use of a favorite illustration. This one was cut from a book, but you might find an appealing design on a greeting card or wrapping paper. The technique is decoupage, which is described in detail on page 78. Next I wanted to decorate the same type of chair with a bit of whimsy.

Fruit design decoupage chair.

I walked around the five-and-ten and the card shop to see if something fired my imagination. I sorted through the display of Meyercord decals and tried to think of an unusual way to use them. They are inexpensive, easy to use, and readily available. However, sticking a decal in the center of a chair back isn't very creative or unusual. I especially liked the border design of growing vines, and I brought it home to play around with. Often when doing decoupage I have created my own climbing vines from cut-out paper leaves to use for plant pedestals. It has been tedious work cutting each tiny

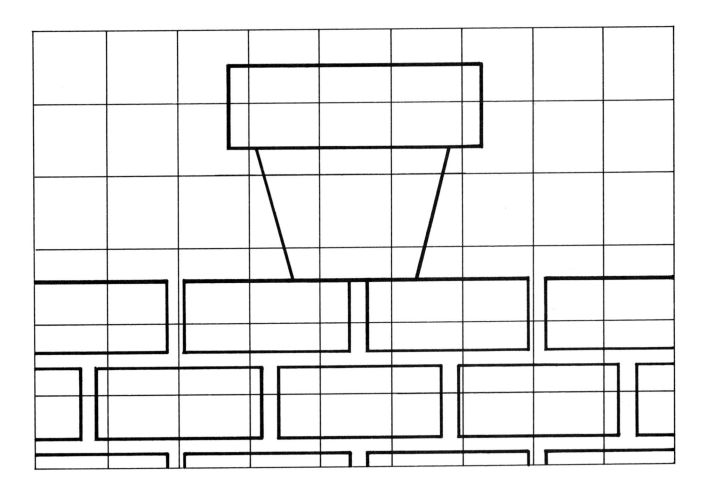

leaf and gluing it in place. Furthermore, it has been difficult to find just the right size for the item in the quantity required. The vine decals offer an alternative to tedious work.

Materials Needed: Semi-gloss or glossy white latex paint, acrylic paint (one small tube each of Cobalt Blue, red oxide or Portrayt, burnt sienna), paintbrush, tracing paper, pencil, masking tape, two-inch sponge brush or stencil brush, one box Meyercord border vine decals, scissors, bowl with warm water, clean dry towel, high-gloss polyurethane varnish, fine sandpaper, brush cleaner.

Sand the chair and paint it with the primer coat of white latex. It will take a few minutes for the paint to dry. Mix enough pale blue paint to cover the entire chair. It takes only a drop or two of the blue mixed with plenty of white to achieve this color. (If you prefer, you can choose another color to match your kitchen.)

Trace the bricks and the flowerpot provided here and enlarge to fit the seat of your chair (see page 146). Place your tracing face down on the seat area and transfer the design by rubbing over the back of the tracing paper with a pencil. The bricks should come down over the front and sides of the chair. Cut strips of masking tape to outline the bricks and flowerpot. Lay these down to outline the areas to be painted and to keep the lines sharply defined.

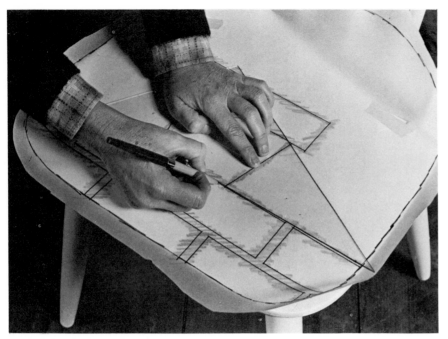

Transfer design to surface of chair seat.

Apply masking tape.

Mix a small amount of paint in a jar or bowl. You will have to determine approximately how much you will need to cover the areas to be painted, but you can mix more if you run out. The combination of two earthy colors, the red oxide shade and the burnt sienna shade, will give the illustration more character than the use of one color. Mix a little bit of white latex with both the red oxide and the burnt sienna acrylic paints.

The bricks are painted with red oxide; the flowerpot is painted with burnt sienna. The color can be brushed on with a two-inch-

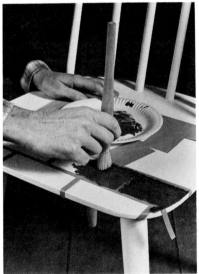

Create brick texture with stencil brush.

Remove tape carefully.

wide sponge brush, but a stencil brush gives texture to the bricks. To use the stencil brush, first brush the paint onto the area, then stipple the surface by holding the brush upright and tapping it up and down. The paint dries almost as soon as it's applied. When the paint is dry, remove the masking tape carefully to avoid smudges.

You might want to plan approximately where the leaves will be placed, but it is not too difficult to work out the placement as you go along. I placed vines where they seemed natural, without any preplanning. As you can see, the leaves extend up and curl around the rung on the back and down and around one leg. I cut off one leaf to place on the bricks as if it had just fallen there. Have some fun with your design, allowing it to interact with the chair. This project required one box of border decals, which cost less than a dollar.

Cut a manageable length of the border decal from the strip it comes on. If you cut a short strip of border and find you want it to extend farther, you can easily add another length of vine to it. Have a pair of scissors handy while placing the decals on the chair. In this way you can work smoothly, cutting the vines to weave and bend and overlap any way at all.

Fill a bowl with warm water. Place the first section of vine in the water for a couple of minutes. The decal will slide away from the paper backing with ease. Slide a small section of backing off and place the decal on the chair before removing the rest of the paper backing. When you are sure it is where you want it, pat the decal down with a clean dry towel to absorb the moisture. Do not rub, because you will wrinkle and remove the decal. Just pat gently. Examine the entire piece to make sure you have smoothed all wrinkles in the decals. When you are satisfied with their placement, let them dry.

A coat of high-gloss polyurethane varnish will give the chair a shiny, bright finish and will protect the design from rubbing away with wear. The acrylic paint is harder to cover with varnish, so it is best to apply more than one coat to compensate for the brick and flowerpot areas. Let each coat dry thoroughly before applying the next. After two or three coats, sand the surface very lightly with fine sandpaper or steel wool to remove any bumpy imperfections on the surface.

When I finished this project I was so pleased that I wanted to think of other ways to use the decals. You might enjoy creating a vase filled with flowers. There are many beautiful decals of practically every kind of flower to choose from. Browse through decal displays for inspiration.

Cut and apply decals. Create the design as you go.

Baby's Dresser Turned Plant Stand

This wicker fold-out baby's dresser was in perfect condition when I began work on it. After it had outlived its original function, it was used to hold extra towels and sheets. I decided it was ripe for another transformation. Pieces like this one, which show up regularly at yard sales, are highly adaptable. They make excellent plant holders when they are swung open, because each section is sturdy and roomy. Low-growing plants can be placed in the compartments below, with larger ones on top. The top can be left open or shut, or you can remove it altogether. I have filled mine with plants, and I keep it on an open porch.

If you find anything made of wicker that's in fairly good condition, grab it. First, wicker items are well designed and versatile. Second, they are durable and, in the case of chairs and sofas, comfortable. Besides all that, wicker furniture never seems to go out of style. You can add cushions in contemporary fabrics to chairs and sofas, paint the wicker from time to time, or, if you're ambitious, stencil a design on some pieces. When painting wicker, you'll find that spray enamel covers best and the job can be done in minutes.

However, spray painting is more expensive than painting by hand. It took a whole can of antique white to give this piece an undercoat.

Materials Needed: One can antique white Krylon spray paint, one tube green artist's oil paint, linseed oil, one piece of glass approximately 9 by 12 inches, palette knife, rubber brayer, tapered artist's brush, Con-Tact paper or vinyl wallcovering (optional), clear spray varnish.

The use of two colors of paint and two different techniques for applying them emphasizes the woven texture of the wicker. Begin by spraying on an undercoat of base color. I used antique white for the undercoat; however, your color scheme will be determined by your taste and the colors available in spray paint. For a wider choice of colors, you might use an undercoat color that you've derived from mixing acrylic color with white latex paint, but you will have to apply it with a brush.

For the topcoat, I chose green because it suggests plants and the outdoors. To prepare the topcoat, squeeze a generous amount of oil paint (in this case, green) on the piece of glass. Add two drops of linseed oil and mix thoroughly with a palette knife. Use the brayer

After spray-painting base coat, use brayer to apply second color.

to roll out the paint until the glass is evenly coated, much like an inking pad. Coat the brayer with paint and roll it over the wicker. The paint will adhere only to the raised areas. Don't worry about applying it perfectly; you can touch it up later. The resulting effect is that of a two-tone basket weave.

The reason for using oil-based rather than acrylic paint is that in order to get the paint to roll on evenly it must be thinned. Oil-based paint thinned by linseed oil remains opaque, but acrylic paint must be thinned with water, and water makes the paint translucent.

Use an artist's tapered brush to paint the trim, edges, and spots where the brayer didn't deposit enough paint. Play around with it until you have achieved the effect you want.

The inside can be painted or lined with Con-Tact paper or vinyl wallcovering. Spray clear varnish inside and out to protect the painted finish. (Krylon makes a clear spray varnish.)

You could also use this kind of piece as a dry bar for occasional parties, on the porch or lawn, for instance. Keep bottles and glasses in the compartments. You might even add casters to the legs for easy transport.

Shopping in Style

Found in the corner of an attic, this abandoned object was quite unattractive in its dusty, grimy condition. But I saw it had potential as a shopping cart, a hanging dried-flower holder, an umbrella stand, or a toy collector. The refurbishing took a minimum of time and effort.

This wicker basket has wooden wheels and stand and a rounded bamboo handle. The woven reed was in perfect condition, but it needed cleaning badly. Soap and water did the trick. After this the wicker was stained with MinWax stain in a dark walnut color. This can be applied with a brush or rag. Acrylic paint was used to decorate the wheels and handle. I stained the interior to match the outside, but you might want to line it with fabric.

Other items to look for that can be treated in the same way are picnic and other kinds of baskets and wicker clothes hampers. When painted, any of these accessories can be used to hold plants. Look for objects that can, with a little stain or paint, change their appearance from drab and inconspicuous to interesting and exciting. And the functional aspect will still be there.

127

Patchwork Cover-up

Don't overlook that plain but sturdy desk chair at a yard sale. If its usefulness is apparent, its plainness can be made less so. I suggest covering it with wallpaper or fabric because the texture and patterns will dominate, minimizing the not overly appealing shape. A table or dresser can be covered in the same way.

This project was fun to do and cost only five dollars. The chair is covered with small, square remnants of printed fabric that were applied with spray adhesive. The pieces of fabric came in a package that I purchased for four dollars in a fabric shop. The package contained enough material to cover the entire chair, including the underside. You might have scraps from sewing projects on hand, or you can buy remnants and choose your own designs and colors. Most of the fabric I used is cotton or flannel. The thin materials work best. Once the chair is completely covered, it looks almost cushioned because of the texture.

Materials Needed: Plenty of remnant fabrics in a variety of colors and patterns, scissors, cardboard or newspaper, fabric spray adhesive (I used 3M Scotch-brand Spra-Ment), roller or rubber brayer (optional), nail polish remover—to clean your hands. (The last is important; nothing else removes the adhesive.)

Begin by cleaning the chair with a dry cloth to remove dust. Spread the pieces of material loosely over the chair. Rearrange colors and patterns to get a general idea of how it will look. It's next to impossible to exercise complete control over the final design, but the finished piece will almost always look good because the project is fail-proof. Once you've covered part of the piece, you'll abandon any plan and simply apply the pieces at random.

Cut many of the fabric pieces into large and small triangles; later you can cut pieces to fit here and there as needed. Spread them face down on a piece of cardboard or newspaper. Spray several pieces of the fabric generously with fabric adhesive. (Because the adhesive is very sticky, the can will clog if you don't follow the directions. Read them carefully before proceeding.) Lift one piece of fabric by a corner and lay it down on one corner of the seat. Smooth it with your hand. It will hold securely. If you don't like the way it looks there, you can easily peel it off and reposition it. The fabric can be lifted and set down again and again if you aren't satisfied while working. To bond these pieces permanently, however, you may have to re-spray the back of them so that they're sufficiently tacky.

Liberally coat patches with spray adhesive. Work on the seat first; it's the easiest.

Continue to attach piece after piece of fabric to the seat. Overlap or butt the fabric where necessary, alternating colors and designs. Next work on the arms and back, leaving the leftover scraps for the legs and other areas not readily seen. Press the fabric down as you work. A roller or rubber brayer may come in handy. If a piece doesn't stay securely, simply lift it, spray with more adhesive, and re-apply.

As the patchwork progresses, stand back from time to time to gain perspective. The project will take on a completely new character with each viewing. This haphazard technique can produce a real surprise piece of furniture. But there are some general design guidelines you might want to follow. Try to balance the colors and patterns. If you are using predominantly earth tones, or dull colors, stick accents of bright yellow or red in places that are not too

Maneuver patches around difficult areas.

prominent. For example, I used a bright yellow fabric with green polka dots, but I used it sparingly and in smaller pieces than those of darker colors.

If you want to dress up this idea, try a taffeta, velvet, and satin combination. For a baby's room, you might consider using delicate rosebud flannel in different colors. What about a calico-and-gingham-covered stool for a sewing room, or suede cloth in earth tones for an unusual chair?

Once the entire object has been covered, turn it around and upside down. Check for any bare spots and cover them with small leftover pieces. This will seal all the edges so they won't ravel and curl after repeated use.

When I finished covering this chair, I couldn't imagine letting anyone sit in it. I think it will be nice in the room of one of my daughters. The clothes that will be piled on it will surely be camouflaged. If you use this technique on a table, have a glass cover cut to fit the top. This will protect the cloth surface and give depth to the design. Glass can be cut to any size and in various thicknesses. Look in the Yellow Pages for a glass-cutter, or ask at your hardware store.

Interior Design

A unique idea for designs on wood comes from my friend Beverly Ellsley's custom-designed kitchen. She has many wooden cabinets in this charming country room and wanted a practical but interesting way to finish the interior doors, walls, shelves, drawers, and so on. The exterior of the cabinets is stained with a green glaze. The same glaze stain was used to pattern the interiors of every storage space in the kitchen, including the broom closet. And the most interesting part of this idea is that every pattern is different. While they may look complicated and tedious to execute, the designs were all done in a haphazard way. Each was created as the printmaker went along, using, as tools, hands, a paintbrush, a sponge, rags, and fingers. These were dipped into the glaze and applied to the surfaces in random patterns.

In order to avoid too strong a contrast between background and pattern, the surfaces were painted tan; then a darker stain was applied over the paint. While the shapes of the patterns are crude, the colors are subtle and the effect is sophisticated. This technique works especially well on the insides of things. The doors open to reveal a fresh visual treat. The interiors look as if they have been lined with decorative paper, when in fact they are finished in a more practical and permanent way. Similar techniques were employed on Early American furniture. Experiment with patterns and designs on a piece of scrap board until you have a feeling for the process. For added protection, all interiors can be given a coat of high-gloss varnish.

Vanity Table and Chair Make-over

Painted white and positioned against a white wall, this little vanity table wasn't getting the attention it deserved tucked away in an old bathroom. Although the white paint was chipping and peeling away to reveal a coat of red beneath, overall the piece was in fairly good shape. The condition of the table, combined with its delicacy, its potential usefulness as a vanity or desk, and the charm of its carved ribbon ornament, inspired me to give it new life. A fresh paint job seemed to be the answer, and a wallpaper design suggested the color scheme. (Wallpaper is a terrific source for decorating ideas and is worth considering for many crafting projects.)

The wallpaper is a vinyl Wall-Tex covering that is predominantly pale blue with white and green detail. Matching fabric is available and can be used to make coordinated curtains or throw-pillow covers.

In painting the vanity table, I wanted to capture the spirit of the wallpaper design as well as use the exact background color. Since the wallpaper is pastel and the pattern delicate, I eliminated green as too strong a color for the vanity. I decided to pick up the pastel blue in the paper for the body of the table; the trim I painted white.

Materials Needed: Semi-gloss or glossy white latex paint, one tube Cobalt Blue acrylic paint, palette knife, scrap piece of cardboard, two-inch-wide paintbrush, tapered artist's brush, brush cleaner, tracing paper, pencil, high-gloss clear varnish, very fine steel wool, clear paste wax, soft clean cloth.

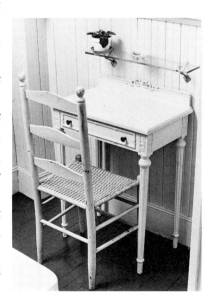

Lightly sand your piece of furniture and prime it with a coat of semi-gloss or glossy white latex paint.

Then mix your background paint color. In this case, a drop of Cobalt Blue acrylic was added to one cup of white latex in a jar. Use a palette knife to mix the color on a piece of cardboard until you obtain the exact color you want. Then keep adding more blue or white paint in your jar, using the color on the cardboard as a guide. When applied to a large area, the color will seem brighter than it does in the jar, so you should mix the paint to look a little paler than you think it should. Do this by adding more white to the mixture.

Now you are ready to apply the background color. When painting a large, flat, dominant area, take the time to do a good job.

136

Keep the paint fairly thin on your brush, and paint in one direction. You will have trouble sanding the surface smooth once it is dry if you've left brush marks going in all directions in the paint. Save some paint for touch-ups if you will be painting the details in another color. Wait until the background color dries before painting the trim with a contrasting color. (Use a tapered artist's brush for details.)

For the matching chair, I used the same pale blue paint color on the background and added a similar ribbon-and-bow design to the back of the chair. You may want to re-create this project by following the directions for painting the vanity. Trace the motif provided here and transfer it to your object by taping the tracing face down on the chair and rubbing a pencil over the back of the tracing paper. Or you can create your own design from your wallpaper or fabric in the same way. Use the design motif on other pieces to coordinate a variety of objects. Acrylic paint is excellent for this kind of work and can be applied with an artist's brush.

To protect the painted surface, give your piece a coat of high-gloss clear varnish. Apply this very carefully and do not overload your brush. (When buying the varnish, be sure it is non-yellowing clear. Sometimes pastel colors such as blue and pink turn slightly green and orange, respectively, if the varnish applied

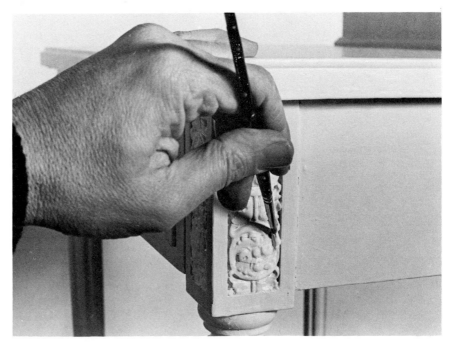

Use small brush to paint details.

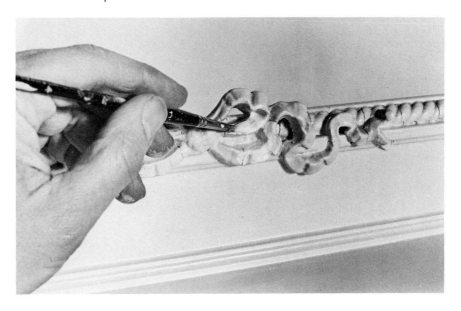

over them has too much yellow in it. However, the protective coating is necessary if you want to use the furniture and keep the new paint looking fresh for a long time.) Brush the varnish over all exposed areas and let it dry thoroughly overnight. I did not apply varnish to the rush seat area of this chair. But if the chair you are working on has a wooden seat, protect this with varnish as well.

Once the varnish is completely dry, lightly rub the surface with a piece of very fine steel wool. Wipe away any steel particles. Apply a coat of clear paste wax, such as that made by Butcher's or Johnson's, and buff the piece with a clean cloth. This once drab, inconspicuous object is now the focal point in my bathroom.

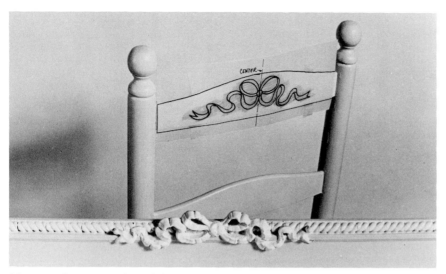

Mount tracing paper on back of chair.

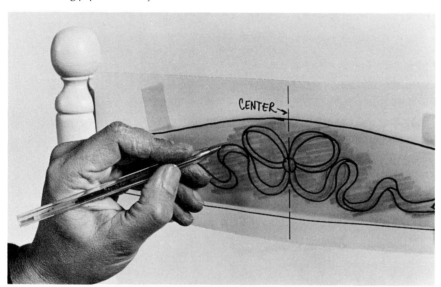

Bow design transferred to back of chair.

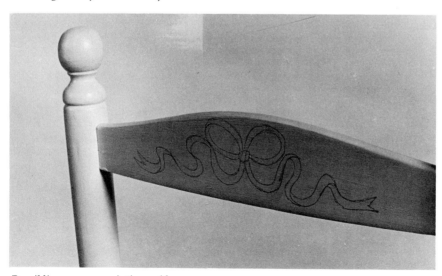

Pencil lines serve as painting guide.

Flowering Table

While prowling in Island Attic Industries, a seconds shop, I came across a small salad plate with a delicate floral design around the rim. Its potential as a design on a round tabletop attracted my attention. Often a small design that interests you can be blown up to serve as decoration on a larger scale. The tabletop I had in mind is six times larger than the plate, and the technique that is appropriate for executing the design on the table is stenciling. Since this project involves enlarging a design, the list of materials needed may seem long. However, if you are using a design that does not require enlargement you can eliminate many of them.

Materials Needed: Heavy grade of sandpaper, finishing sander (if an old finish must be removed), semi-gloss antique white latex paint, two-and-a-half-inch all-purpose brush, original design (could be from a plate, poster, or even sheets), tracing paper, graph paper, compass, ruler, rubber cement, stencil brush and paper, X-Acto or utility knife, acrylic paint in desired colors, palette knife or other flat utensil, high-gloss or satin-finish varnish, brush cleaner, very fine sandpaper or steel wool, clear furniture paste wax, soft cloth.

Sand off original finish.

Repaint surface of table.

The round table used here is a heavy maple game table with a checkerboard design burnished in the center of the top. Having been used for many years, it was scratched and in need of refinishing, but restoration didn't seem to be the answer because it wasn't a very interesting table to begin with and I felt that the heaviness was overwhelming for the room in which I wanted to place it.

If you have a similar item and would like to overhaul it completely, the old finish should be removed. This is not always necessary, but it does make the surface more receptive to a new finish. No messy remover was used, because it quickly became apparent that the old finish would come off easily with the aid of a

144

Fill grooves and defects with wood filler.

finishing sander. (No home workshop should be without an electric finishing sander; it makes this kind of job a snap.) The base of the table was sanded less diligently with a hand sanding block and a coarse grade of sandpaper.

Next, I gave the table a base coat of semi-gloss antique white latex paint. When this was dry, I added a second coat. At this point, I realized that the burnished lines of the checkerboard could not be covered with paint and would have to be filled. This step is best done before painting, but since the job was this far along, the wood filler was applied on top of the painted surface. When the filler was dry, I sanded it flush and applied another coat of paint. Preparing furniture to receive decoration can be tedious, but the more care that is taken, the better the results. I have to remind myself of this every so often.

To transfer and enlarge a plate design, begin by dry-mounting a piece of tracing paper to a portion of the plate. To dry-mount the paper, coat it with rubber cement and let the cement dry before placing the paper on the plate. Securing the tracing paper to the plate in this way allows you to trace a perfect outline. If the design contains a repeat pattern, as it does here, you only need to trace one

Trace design and remove paper from plate.

Tracing paper mounted on curved surface.

section. The plate design I used is provided here, so if you wish to use it you should begin by tracing directly from the book.

To enlarge the design easily, glue the tracing over a piece of graph paper. Rule over the lines using a felt-tip marking pen and straightedge so that you can see the design and grid together. Number each square down and across for easy reference when you're enlarging the design.

Next you will need to figure out how large to blow up the design in relation to your tabletop. Draw a circle around the design, using the plate as a template. (If you are using the design from this book, use a compass.) Measure the diameter of the circle. Measure the diameter of your tabletop. Divide the diameter of the tabletop by

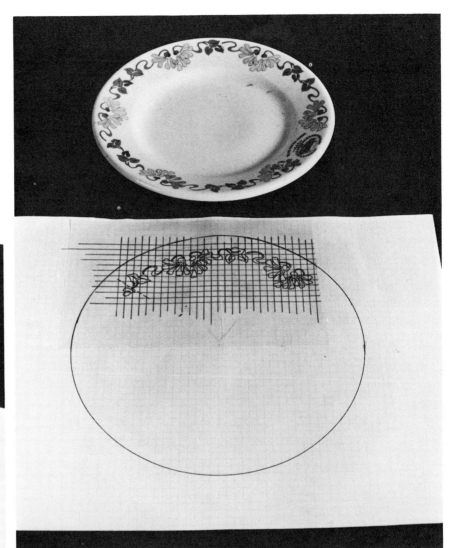

Draw circle around design with compass.   *Draw grid on flower design.*

the diameter of your drawn circle to determine the "enlargement factor," or the number of times to enlarge the design. On a new sheet of graph paper, set up an expanded grid. The length of the sides of each square should equal the length of the sides of the original grid squares multiplied by the enlargement factor.

Number the squares on your large grid to correspond to the squares on the smaller grid, and copy the design square by square onto the new grid. This is not as difficult as it may sound. When you've enlarged the entire design, place a sheet of transparent stencil paper over it. Stencil paper with a waxed backing works best because it grips the tabletop while you work. The chances of any paint seeping under the paper are thereby minimized, and sharp, clean outlines are guaranteed. (See "Sources for Supplies" at the back of this book for a supplier of stenciling equipment.) With an

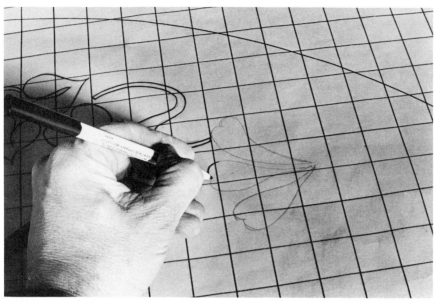

Scale design up to size.

X-Acto or utility knife, go over the outlines of each element of the design. Here, tendrils, petals, leaves, etc. are all cut out individually to make the stencil.

When this is done, lay the stencil on the table and outline the cut-out areas in pencil so that you can see how the design will look. If the design doesn't fit comfortably around the table, adjust the spacing of the elements.

Mix your paint colors carefully, taking care to mix enough of each at one time to finish the job. The acrylic colors are best because there is a wide variety to choose from. They dry quickly and can be used either straight from the tube or mixed together to create colors that match your decor. When purchasing your paint, consider buying a tube of white acrylic paint as well. It always comes in

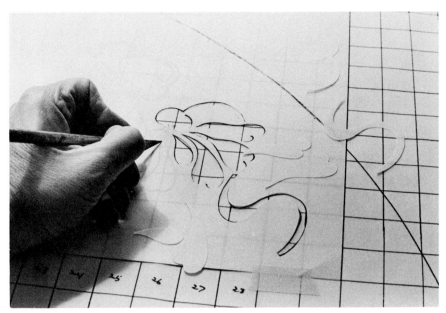

Place stencil paper over design and cut out with sharp blade.

handy for creating pastel colors or lightening very intense colors. A palette knife is indispensable for mixing acrylic paint and is worth the investment. However, other flat utensils, such as a butter knife, a popsicle stick, or a putty knife, can be used in a pinch.

Position the cut-out stencil sheet on the tabletop. If it doesn't have a waxed backing, you will have to secure it in place with masking tape so that it doesn't slip while you are stenciling. Use a stipple brush, made especially for stenciling. (Stipple brushes come in various sizes; medium will do for work on this scale.) Dip the brush into the paint and then tap it a few times on a scrap piece of paper to remove excess paint. Stencil with a minimum of paint on the brush. It is best to apply the paint a little at a time. Hold the brush straight up and down and lightly tap the paint onto the area. When you reach the edge of the design, tap from the edge inward so that excess paint does not accumulate at the edges. Let the paint dry on each area, then apply a second coat in the same way. Work on one section of the design at a time. Let each section dry thoroughly before laying the stencil sheet over it in order to do the next section. Apply one color all the way around before moving on to the next color. Save a little paint of each color for touch-ups.

When you peel the stencil sheet away from the surface for the last time, you will be in for a surprise. I find that the results of stenciling always amaze me. The projects look so professional and the designs so crisply executed that I am inspired to do more.

To protect the surface and make it glow, varnish the entire piece with either high-gloss or satin-finish varnish. The shiny high-gloss finish has a contemporary look; the low-luster satin finish is more traditional in feeling. I prefer the low luster for antique furniture and the high gloss for more fanciful pieces, such as this. However, you

Stencil design on tabletop.

Original plate and enlarged design on table.

can experiment with both, since it takes about three coats to cover the paint adequately. Buy pint-size cans for this purpose. Begin with the high-gloss finish, which will give your table a hard, clear protective covering. Let it dry thoroughly, then apply a coat of the satin on top of this. When that coat dries, if you find you preferred the glossy, simply make the last coat high-gloss. Don't forget to give the base and underside of the table a varnished finish as well. This overall finish will protect the table against moisture and the warping that is associated with it.

When the varnish is completely dry, sand the surface very lightly with fine sandpaper or rub over the surface with very fine steel wool. Treat the table with clear paste wax and buff it to a shine with a soft cloth.

Seed Cabinet Cover-up

I have had this seed cabinet for many years. The drawers are ill-fitting, and once they are removed it is nearly impossible to restore them to their rightful places. However, it's a great-looking old piece, and I thought it should be salvaged. At one point I had added my own coat of black paint to several preceding coats, so the first step seemed to be to strip the cabinet down. My plan was to paste the front of a seed packet to each drawer. A coat of varnish would bring out the luster of the wood and coat the packets. This plan turned out to be one of those plans that is better imagined than carried out.

I took the piece to a commercial stripping establishment. Even after several chemical baths the paint wouldn't budge; I was told this sometimes happens with black paint. I took the cabinet home and got out the Strypeeze paint and varnish remover and my electric finishing sander. An hour later I had only one drawer stripped down to the bare wood. (If it hadn't been such a nice day I couldn't have labored that long for so little result!) Unfortunately—or fortunately, depending on how you look at it—what I uncovered was not interesting old wood but what looked like unfinished plywood.

The original seed cabinet.

Stripping attempted and abandoned.

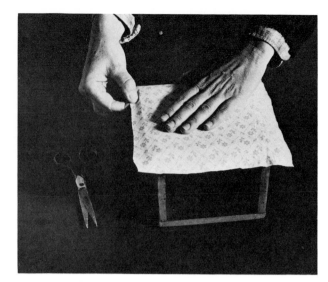

Glue fabric to surface; trim corners and fold under.

I decided to cover the drawers and frame instead—with a delicate fabric. You can cover any piece of furniture this way. I used Elmer's Glue-All for permanent bonding. If you think you might want to change the fabric from time to time, use a spray adhesive such as Spra-Ment made by 3M. You will be able to lift the fabric away from the piece and attach a replacement.

Materials Needed: Enough fabric to cover the item, Elmer's Glue-All or Spra-Ment fabric adhesive, staple gun and staples (optional), scissors, pencil, ruler, sponge, nail polish remover for cleaning hands (if spray adhesive is used).

Any detailed areas that will not be covered with fabric must be painted before you apply the fabric. You might choose paint to match the background of the fabric. The fabric used here was designed by Laura Ashley and is a delicate pink floral print on a white background.

If you are covering a piece that has regular dimensions, simply add a little extra to each measurement to allow for turning the pieces of cloth in or under where required. For extra strength, staple the fabric under the furniture. This cabinet is old and the dimensions are not standardized. No two drawers are exactly the same size. In order to measure correctly, I placed each section of the cabinet on the fabric, marked the size with a pencil, and cut, leaving a half-inch allowance on all sides. If you are doing sections of a printed fabric, try to cut them so that the pattern matches from one piece to another where the edges will meet. When buying the fabric, purchase a bit extra so you will have enough for matching.

154

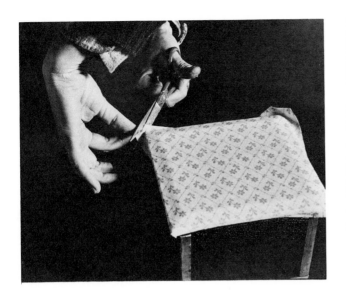 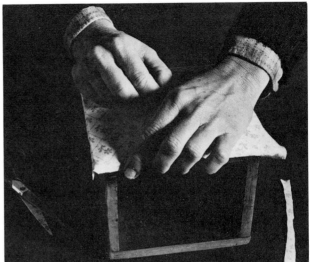

If you use white glue, such as Elmer's, rather than the spray adhesive, dilute it slightly with water so that you can brush it onto a section of the furniture. Place the fabric on the glued area and pull the edges outward to smooth out wrinkles and keep it taut. Be sure the pattern in the fabric is straight.

When working with glue and fabric, wash your hands from time to time so you don't stain the fabric. Have a damp sponge handy to wipe up excess that may ooze out from under the edges of the fabric. After the piece is completely covered, consider spraying it with Scotchgard Fabric Protector to retard soiling. Fabrics that have been mill-treated with Scotchgard will say so on the back. Look for this when purchasing your material. Other fabrics, such as polished cotton, have not been treated, but they can be sponge cleaned. For the most part, fabric coverings applied to furniture do not wear as well as wallpaper coverings, but they do look sensational. A Parson's table that has been covered with fabric to be used as an end table or coffee table can be protected by a piece of glass or Plexiglas cut to fit over the top.

If you are covering a dresser with fabric, begin by removing the knobs and drawers and work on each section separately. Make sure that the fabric pattern matches from one drawer to the next, as well as the connection at sides and top. You might want to look for unusual knobs to replace the old ones.

Butterfly Cabinet

This piece of furniture is true junk. Although it has been used for many years as a record cabinet, its original identity is a mystery, and I no longer remember the circumstances under which it came into my house. It is poorly designed, made of cheap wood, and was in the process of falling apart when I began work on it. Despite these obvious drawbacks, my daughter thought it was perfect for holding records and a stereo, so I decided it was worth trying to enhance its appearance. There are lots of odds and ends that aren't pretty but can serve a function. It challenges the imagination to think of a way to decorate and make something of this sort of piece.

When visiting San Francisco I bought a large paper butterfly kite in Chinatown. The bold, colorful design seemed a natural for giving a decorative focus to the cabinet. The thinness of the paper used for these kites requires that they be handled with care, but it also makes them perfect for decoupage—once the wooden frame is removed, of course! In removing the frame I ripped the paper a bit, but I was able to mend it as I glued it to the cabinet. You will be able to find kites similar to the one I used in novelty stores in your area.

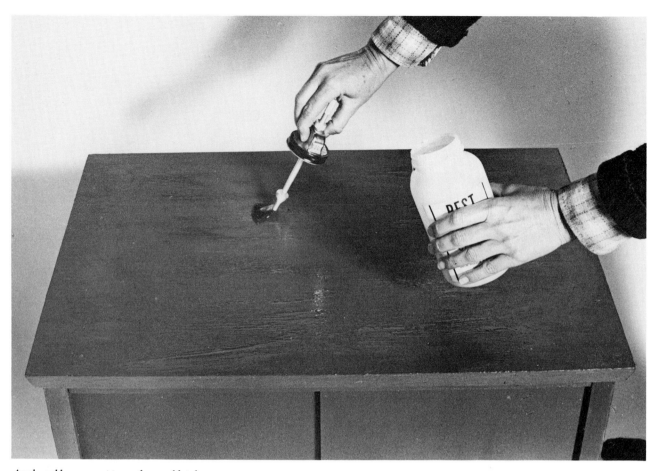

Apply rubber cement to surface and let dry.

Materials Needed: Large paper kite or other design, acrylic paint, rubber cement, rubber-cement thinner, tracing paper, brayer, rubber-cement pickup (optional), Elmer's Glue-All, brush, high-gloss indoor wood varnish, very fine sandpaper, brush cleaner.

It wasn't necessary to remove the paint from the surface of the cabinet. A fast overall hand sanding smoothed surface blemishes before a new coat of paint was applied. For the background color, I chose a bright cherry red that can hold its own against the intense colors of the butterfly design. Acrylic paint can be used here right from the tube. Since it is quite thick, you will occasionally need to add a drop of water to your brush for an even application. Remember to remove knobs and hardware (when possible) before you begin to paint. Clean the brush with hot water when you have finished painting.

The butterfly, or any illustration made on thin paper, is best mounted with rubber cement. White glue is too thick to use with a lightweight paper, and it increases the hazard of ripping. Also, a design mounted with rubber cement can be removed with rubber-cement thinner and re-applied if it is laid incorrectly.

Place cemented paper butterfly on slip sheet.

Coat both the back of your design and the entire surface to which it will be attached with rubber cement. (Don't worry about covering your furniture with rubber cement. When it has dried you only have to rub your finger over the excess to remove it.) Let the rubber cement dry on each surface. To position the butterfly before securing it, use a piece of tracing paper as a slip sheet. The tracing paper will not adhere to the rubber cement. Place the tracing paper between the paper decoration and the furniture surface and position the decoration accurately. Place one corner of the paper design directly onto the rubber-cement-coated surface of the furniture and press down so that it adheres to the surface. Now, slowly pull the tracing paper out from under the design as you press and smooth the butterfly or other decoration onto the surface. If you've applied the design and you find that it is crooked or wrinkled, do not try to pull it up all at once. Put a few drops of rubber-cement thinner right on top of one edge of the decoration. This will seep through and dissolve the rubber cement beneath. The paper design will then lift

159

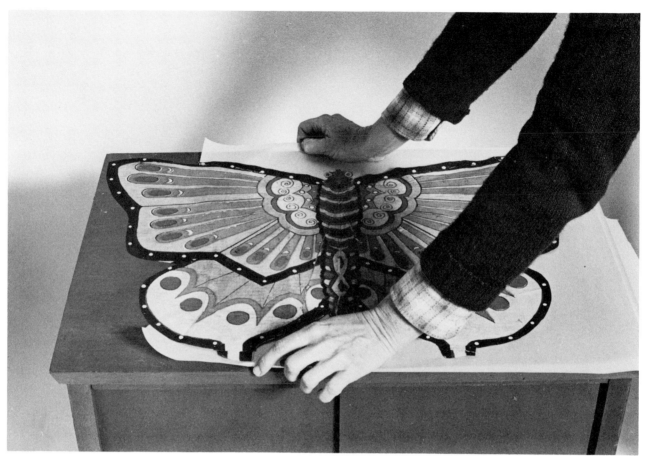

Dry-mount butterfly by slipping sheet out slowly.

easily, and you can keep applying more thinner to the underside of the design as you peel it away. To reposition, you will first have to apply more rubber cement to the paper decoration and the furniture surface. As you can see, it is better to try to do it as perfectly as possible the first time.

Once the decoration is cemented down, smooth over all areas with a brayer. Take care to avoid tearing the paper. You can use your fingers or a rubber-cement pickup, which is like a flat, rectangular eraser, to remove the excess rubber cement around the design. (This "eraser" is available where art supplies are sold.) Work outward from the edges of the paper toward the edges of the furniture.

When decorating like this, you have to be careful about the finish that you apply over the design, because some colored inks will run if varnish is applied to them directly. Most printing inks used for book illustrations or greeting cards can be covered successfully with varnish. However, since I didn't know what kind of ink was used to print this kite design, caution was in order. If you are working with something similar, such as a magazine or newspaper print, you can ensure that the color will not run in the following way:

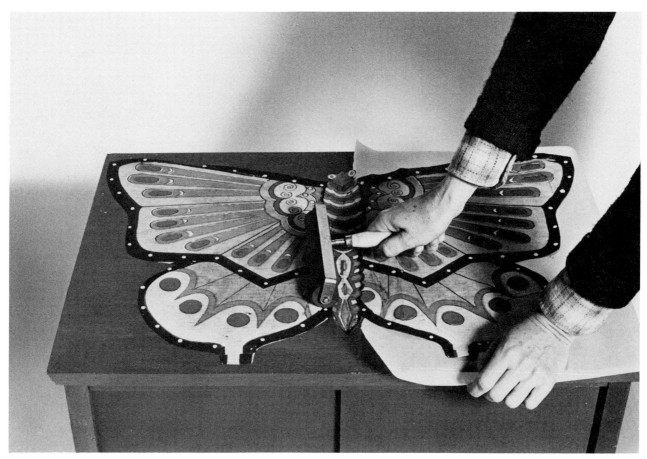

Use brayer to secure paper.

Dilute a tablespoonful of Elmer's Glue-All with a few drops of water and stir the mixture until its consistency is even. Brush the mixture over the paper design. The surface will be white and streaked, but the print will not smudge. Let the glue dry. It will be clear. If it isn't, wait a few minutes longer. Eventually the glue coating will dry transparent and the print will be set. Now you can varnish over the design without fear of smudging or removing the colors.

High-gloss varnish gives this piece a shiny, contemporary look which is perfect for its function and design. The legs, which were originally painted black, are also coated with varnish. Apply several coats over the entire surface, letting each coat dry between applications. After three coats, sand the surface lightly. Then apply two or three more coats of varnish to further protect and submerge the design.

For added interest, replace old hardware with more interesting finds from the hardware store, junk shop, or five-and-ten. Other decorative ideas include bits and pieces of memorabilia arranged in a collage that covers the entire piece of furniture, comic-book pages, newspaper items of interest, play programs, or a poster of your favorite hero.

Piano Bench Tabled

This was a piano bench in search of a piano. At one time the two became separated, and the bench was relegated to the attic to serve as a repository for old songbooks and long-forgotten homework papers. The fabric covering on the seat lid was now mildewed, and the hinges were hanging on by one screw each. Even without its piano, though, such a piece can be useful and attractive—as a small window bench or even a coffee table.

After much consideration as to what might be an appropriate function and crafting technique for this bench, a thought came to me. The bench had come from the seashore house of friends. The two small boys and their parents like to beachcomb, and all summer they bring buckets and buckets of shells and stones home from the beach. The bench could serve double-duty as a window seat and a cache for their collection of shells. From this came the idea for the motif and the crafting technique I would use. It seemed appropriate to create a scene of beach grasses, low flowering shrubs, and other seashore life along the top of the bench. For this I used some paper cutouts as well as some homemade blades of grass that I painted and cut out to fit my beach scene. Illustrations snipped from books, wrapping paper, and wallpaper would have worked equally well as design elements. As far as uses to which such a piece can be put, the storage space beneath the seat is an excellent place to stash sewing materials or hobby supplies for easy access. Devise a design to fit your needs, and use the directions that follow as your guidelines.

Cut flowers out with cuticle scissors.

Materials Needed: Enamel spray paint (in this case, black), brush, sandpaper, cuticle scissors, paper decorations, Elmer's Glue-All, sponge, varnish, brush cleaner, fine and medium grade sandpaper (3M WetorDry No. 200 and No. 400), very fine steel wool, wood filler (if needed), clear furniture paste wax.

Begin by sanding the furniture so that it is smooth and ready for painting. This piece was scratched and gouged, and the lid was full of tack holes from the fabric "upholstery," so I began by plugging the crevices with wood filler. When the wood filler was dry, I sanded the surface with medium-grade sandpaper to prepare it for painting. To obtain a high-gloss effect, it is best to use spray paint. For most of the projects in this book, I've advised for the sake of economy that you paint by hand. However, this bench is small enough to make spray painting a feasible alternative. It will take a full can to cover a piece this size. I used flat black spray paint for a background that would contrast strongly with my seaside flora. (Read about spray painting in "Tips on Repairing and Preparing" before proceeding.)

Cut out all the pieces you will need for your design. For fine cutting, I recommend sharp cuticle scissors. Rearrange the pieces until you are happy with the final placement. Take off one piece at a time and coat the back with Elmer's Glue-All. Replace the piece, press firmly, and pat it down with a damp sponge. The sponge will pick up any excess glue. Once all the designs have been glued in place and the glue is dry, apply a coat of varnish over the entire piece. I used a high-gloss polyurethane varnish here, but if you prefer a low-luster finish, use a matte- or satin-finish indoor wood varnish. To cover the paper appliqués sufficiently, you will need

Glue cutouts down. Use sponge to pat off excess glue.

Varnish entire surface at least five times.

about five coats of varnish. Let each coat dry thoroughly before applying the next. After three or four coats, sand lightly with fine sandpaper. After you have applied the final coat, rub gently over the entire piece with very fine steel wool. A final protective coating of clear furniture paste wax, buffed, will give the surface a soft glow and the design will seem to be one with the painted surface.

You might want to finish off the storage space beneath the lid by painting it a contrasting color or lining it with paper or fabric. Or you could open up the storage space and use it for display by replacing the wood lid with a lucite lid cut to fit. Coordinate the exterior decorations with the objects to be displayed inside.

Sea Gulls for an Outdoor Table

Round metal umbrella tables stand rusting in many backyards, the umbrellas having worn out long before the tables. The large flat surface lends itself to a variety of designs, and it is easy to paint or stencil on the metal. A coat or two of varnish will keep the painted design from deteriorating.

Living in a sea town, I'm often inspired by the designs found in nature. Sea gulls are beautiful and graphic with their outspread wings. I based my design on soaring sea gulls and used the stenciling technique to execute it. When planning a design, it is a good idea to make a drawing first so that you can get an idea of what the finished piece will look like.

Materials Needed: Heavy-duty sandpaper, finishing sander (if you have a lot of rust to remove) or sanding block, Royal Blue Krylon spray paint, stencil paper, X-Acto knife, stencil brush, two-inch-wide paintbrush, white acrylic paint, small tube of yellow

A rusty surface must be sanded thoroughly.

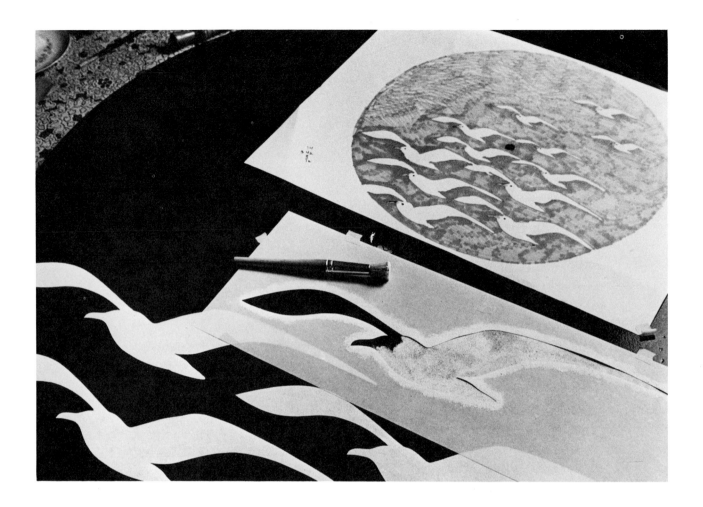

acrylic paint and another of black, high-gloss polyurethane varnish, brush cleaner.

Begin by removing any rust with good heavy-duty sandpaper. This can be done with a finishing sander or by hand with a sanding block. Once the surface is smooth, apply the background color with spray paint. This project may require several coats, depending on the condition of your table and the color you choose. A dark color will cover in fewer coats than a pastel color.

Scale the design provided here to fit your tabletop (see page 146 for how to enlarge designs). Then lay a sheet of stencil paper over the scaled design and cut the stencil by tracing the outline of the sea gull with an X-Acto knife. Place the stencil in position on the tabletop and make a penciled outline of the gull.

To attain clear, crisp outlines, stipple the inside edge with a stencil brush, taking a small amount of white acrylic paint onto the brush and tapping the paint onto the table with an up-and-down movement of the brush. Fill in the rest of the large areas with a regular brush. Go over and over the white areas until they are bright white, with none of the blue showing through. There should be no differentiating boundaries where the sea gulls overlap. The interplay of white shapes creates a strong graphic effect. If you want to

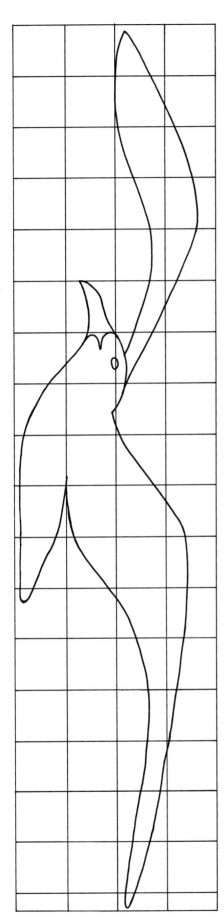

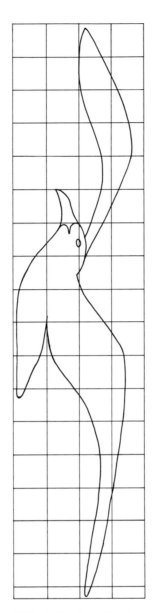

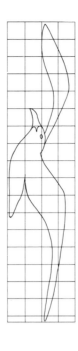

Sea-gull illustration is used in three sizes.

add detail to the wings, this can be done with gray paint.

Once the white paint is dry, fill in the beaks with yellow acrylic applied over the white. Dots of black paint serve as eyes. These will dry quickly.

To protect the painted surface from wear and tear and the weather, coat the tabletop, underside, and base with high-gloss polyurethane varnish. The more coats you apply, the greater the protection for your table. Five coats should do it. If you have outdoor director chairs, you can buy canvas seats and backs in royal blue and use your sea-gull stencil to transfer the gull design to the canvas. This washable material takes the acrylic paint very well, and the design will be permanent.

Marbleizing a Buffet the Lazy Way

Marbleizing is a technique for simulating marble with oil paint on wood. The process seems easy enough to understand, and the materials are available in art-supply stores, but to achieve results that one would consider acceptable is not so easy. In fact, to create a believable *faux* marble effect you should either be a real artist or bring plenty of time, patience, and practice to the task. If the results are not up to one's expectations, an otherwise good piece of furniture can be ruined. This project employs a simple, fail-safe method for attaining the look of marble.

I have an old buffet that was badly scratched on the top, although the rest of it was in fairly good shape. I took it to a commercial stripper, who wouldn't touch it because its lacquered finish promised to put up a good deal of resistance. Thus I had to select a technique for covering the finish rather than removing it. The curves of the buffet reminded me of the shapes of many pieces of marble I've seen.

With this in mind, I sanded down the top with a finishing sander and applied a base coat of white enamel point. But when the moment came to put marbleizing oil paint to furniture, a voice within me cried, Stop! Sometimes this happens even to the so-called experts. Everyone eventually meets his or her match, and in this case marbleizing was mine.

I turned instead to the wide selection of beautiful marble-patterned papers sold for binding books and for other kinds of crafting projects. Wallpaper is also available in similar designs. Any piece of furniture can be completely covered if it is in disrepair and you don't want to bother stripping, staining, or painting it. The variety of coverings to choose from is endless, and you can create any mood you want. The oil paints were put away before any damage could be done.

Materials Needed: Enough book-binding paper or wallpaper (Wall-Tex vinyl wallcovering, in this case) to cover the piece you're working on, 3M Scotch-brand Spra-Ment spray adhesive, scissors, razor blade or cuticle scissors. If the paper you're using isn't heavy, like vinyl paper, or coated, you may want to protect it with varnish. For this you will need varnish, a brush, and brush cleaner.

For this project, the rim of the buffet top was painted with acrylic paint to match the wood finish. When you are ready to cover the piece with the paper, begin at the top. To cut the paper to fit, I turned my buffet upside down on the paper and traced all around the top. Then I cut out the piece of paper and sprayed the back of it

After mounting paper, trim edges with sharp blade.

with adhesive. Carefully lay the cut-out piece of paper on the area to be covered. If you haven't placed it precisely where you want it, peel the piece away and reposition it. With white glue the bonding is more permanent, making planning and accuracy the first time around more important. Excess paper around the edges can be trimmed with a razor blade or cuticle scissors. The vinyl paper is quite thick, and I found that cuticle scissors made it easier to get a close, clean cut.

Next, measure and cut pieces for other sections. Here, the insides of the doors are covered to match the top. Tape a piece of tracing paper to the insides of the doors and make an outline of the areas to be covered. Use this tracing as your guide for cutting the lining paper. The drawers can be lined also. Measure all sides accurately, cut out each section, and glue in place. The vinyl paper doesn't require a protective varnish, because it is durable and can be cleaned with a damp sponge.

Admittedly, we don't wind up with marble to fool the eye, but we do have a one-of-a-kind buffet—transformed for the cost of paper and adhesive—that looks quite handsome.

Make templates with plain paper.

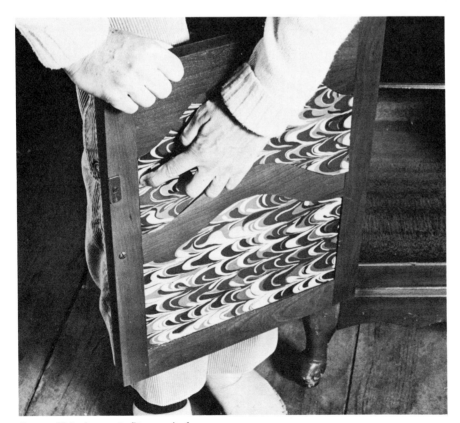

Cut marbleized paper to fit recess in door.

For Further Reading

Antiques: Professional Secrets for the Amateur by Michel Doussy. New York: Quadrangle, 1971.

The Art of the Painted Finish for Furniture and Decoration by Isabel O'Neil. New York: William Morrow and Co., 1971.

Fabulous Furniture Decorations by Leslie Linsley. New York: Thomas Y. Crowell, 1978.

Furniture Decoration by Charles Hallett. Newton Centre, Mass.: Charles T. Branford Publishers, 1956.

Sources for Supplies

Most of the crafting materials used for the projects in this book are readily available in hardware or hobby and art-supply stores. However, some items may be hard to find in your area. The following suppliers provide mail-order services and, in some cases, catalogs that are quite extensive.

Art Supplies

Charrette
31 Olympia Avenue
Woburn, MA 01801

Arthur Brown, Inc.
2 West 46th Street
New York, NY 10036

Caning and Weaving Materials

The H. H. Perkins Company
10 South Bradley Road
Woodbridge, CT 06525

Decoupage Supplies

American Handicrafts Company
P.O. Box 2911
Fort Worth, TX 76101

Connoisseur Studio, Inc.
P.O. Box 7187
Louisville, KY 40207

Hazel Pearson
4128 Temple City Boulevard
Rosemead, CA 91770

O-P Craft Company
425 Warren Street
Sandusky, OH 44870

Fabric

Fabrications
146 East 56th Street
New York, NY 10022

Fabrications
114 Newbury Street
Boston, MA 02116

General Craft Supplies

Boycan's Craft Supplies
Mail Order Division
P.O. Box 897
Sharon, PA 16146

J. L. Hammett Company
Hammett Place
Braintree, MA 02184

The Craftool Company, Inc.
1421 West 240th Street
Harbor City, CA 90710

Hardware

Albert Constantine & Sons, Inc.
2050 Eastchester Road
Bronx, NY 10461

Stencil Supplies

Stencil Magic
8 West 19th Street
New York, NY 10011

Veneer

Bob Morgan Woodworking Supplies
915 East Kentucky Street
Louisville, KY 40204